ALL IN

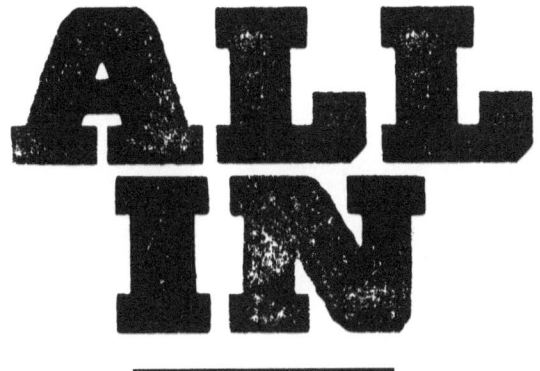

ALL IN

Grabbing Hold of the One
Who Makes Life Count

Kip Gaines & William Dew

Copyright © 2022 Kip Gaines & William Dew

Illustrations and chart design by Kip Gaines, Diana Gaines, and David Dew.

Cover and interior design by Stephanie Spino.

Special thanks to Victoria Dew, Neil and Shanna Barberio, Greg and Valerie Iseral, and Chris Bender for their insight and editing.

For more information, visit: kipgaines.com.

Printed in the United States of America

ISBN: 979-8-218-01489-6 (Paperback)

979-8-218-01490-2 (Ebook)

Contents

Forward

This work is a spiritual journey, an account of a lifetime being *all in*. The truism of this account is the often-overlooked mandate of physical action. As it says in the Gospel of James: *If a brother or sister is naked and destitute of daily food, and one of you says to them, "Depart in peace, be warmed and filled," but you do not give them the things which are needed for the body, what does it profit? Thus, also faith by itself, if it does not have works, is dead.*

For my father, it was to sell a promising and successful business and give up a racing career. We moved to Texas to be missionaries. Not the modern kind. The old school kind. I spent some days hungry, encountered dysentery, disease, war, and poverty. Why? Because my old man was *all in*. My mother was *all in*. This book will tell her story, but I will give a taste of what kind of woman she is. Shortly after a major brain hemorrhage, she began her riskiest work in the Middle East. What had my parents figured out?

"Until one is committed, there is hesitancy, the chance to draw back, always ineffectiveness. Concerning all acts of initiative and creation, there is one elementary truth the ignorance of which kills countless ideas and splendid plans that the moment one definitely commits oneself, then providence moves too. All sorts of things occur to help one that would never otherwise have occurred. A whole stream of events issues from the decision, raising in one's favor all manner of unforeseen incidents, meetings and material assistance which no man could have dreamed would have come his way. Whatever you can do or dream you can, begin it. Boldness has genius, power, and magic in it. Begin it now."—Goethe

At the time of this writing, I have made it around the sun 41 times. I was in my first war zone at eight years old. As a prophecy I think, I cut the tip of my finger in half when we were in Southern Belize. We were twelve hours in any direction from medical care. So, my parents took me to the British Paras who were fighting Guatemalan Guerrillas at the time. They patched me right up. I learned then that men with guns and medicine can do good in places where such things could not otherwise exist. I grew up and became one of those men. I joined the Army and earned a Green Beret. I went to conflicts in Iraq, Central America, and Afghanistan. I saw beauty in the world and harshness in the elements. I wanted to test myself, so I went to guide school, climbed all over the world, and commercial fished in Alaska. I wanted to build things, so I became a carpenter. I wanted to help the hopeless, so I learned Medicine. I have had the opportunity to practice said art on five continents. Currently, I am still practicing as a Flight Paramedic.

The greatest of these things I have learned, or should I say am learning, is love. I was blessed along the way to find my soulmate, Joanna Gaines. I was blessed with three children Paige, Talia, and Leonidas. I was blessed with the best family and friends anyone could ever ask for. I was and am blessed by God. I am *all in*. After reading this work, I hope you will also choose that path.

Nick Gaines

A Word from Will

Life can be confusing. It's not easy to navigate all the hurt, disappointment, and desperate questions gnawing at our souls. But once in a while, we have one of those moments.

You know what I mean. Those moments when you read or hear words that cut through the confusion. All of a sudden, you get it. Your perspective becomes clearer, and things make more sense.

I love those moments.

Surprisingly, these piercing truths usually aren't complex. Looking back, even the most profound revelations are rather simple, even tangible. So incredibly simple, we wonder how we didn't see it before. So tangible, it's as if the truth had always been in our hearts if we ever dared to dig down deep enough. When these truths fall into place, like they were meant to be there, we feel empowered to walk with a little more confidence.

The first time I heard Kip Gaines speak, I was a hungry teenager searching for purpose and direction. I had no idea a summer training program at Youth With A Mission (YWAM) would so alter the course of my life. Kip, one of the teachers, was funny, genuine, and hooked my short attention span. Most importantly, his insight sparked several of those moments. Through Kip's teachings, I saw the Bible, the world, and my purpose in life much clearer. I suddenly understood answers to deep questions I could never quite articulate.

Unlike other speakers I've heard, Kip never forced his teachings. He challenged me and the other students to ask questions, search out the scriptures, and confirm his assertions aligned with the Bible. As I accepted his challenge, the principles he laid out became more than good teaching. They helped solidify the foundation of my worldview. This new understanding empowered me to live a life more like the heroes of the Bible.

Of course, I still have questions, problems, even tragedies. Life is still confusing at times. However, with a clearer perspective, or framework, I'm better equipped to sort out the mess. Kip's teachings helped me to live in peace, despite the chaotic world around me. Are you excited?

I'm excited because I know what you are about to read. When you grab a hold of and apply the Biblical principles in this book, they will fundamentally shift how you see, process, and interact with the world around you. In other words, they will revolutionize your life. My life is proof.

Are you excited yet?

That summer training program changed my life. Since then, I've heard Kip teach dozens of times, and we've become great friends. From teacher, to mentor, to close friend, Kip continues to inspire and challenge me through how he lives. In his victories and struggles, I've watched him hold God's hand and practice the revelation he teaches. It's my great honor to help him share these teachings with readers like you!

Before we go any further, I want to explain my role. Regarding co-authorship, I have three main contributions. First, to make Kip's teachings more readable. If you've had the privilege of hearing Kip speak, you know he's an anointed teacher, but simply transcribing his teachings or notes would not be an easy read.

Second, more than reading words, I hope readers experience and hear Kip's voice. If these teachings are a reminder, I hope you find yourself back in the classroom where you first heard them. May God refresh these powerful revelations and draw you closer. If you haven't yet had this privilege, I pray you hear Kip's humble, sincere heart, that exudes an earnest love for both God and others.

Third, as these chapters were discussed, debated, and refined, Kip insisted we include some of my personal additions as well. That's how it should be, right? There are too many people (even Christians) focused on making a name for themselves, building their own kingdoms, too intimidated to invest in the next generation. The Biblical precedent is to raise up disciples to go further than us. Kip's encouragement and challenges help me walk closer with God. Truthfully, the concepts in this book are so ingrained in my mind, they are now my own convictions. My perspective and additions simply add clarity to the truth which Kip and I hope to invest in others—like you.

This brings me to my mission: to share this truth with as many as possible. From the start, Kip wasn't concerned about publishing anything. But as you'll soon see, these teachings are much too valuable to not share. This world needs more lives revolutionized by the Truth.

I'm excited. What you're about to read changed my life. If you are hungry, willing, and faithful to apply what you read, it will change yours too.

Will Dew

A Word from Kip

This book is dedicated to **you**, the reader. The most precious thing you have is your time, and we do not take that lightly. Each page has been prayed over for you to receive what God has for you! I pray you will receive His anointing as you fellowship with God while reading through these pages.

I want to take a moment to recognize the investment of all those who contributed to these pages. I'm so grateful.

First of all, I want to give thanks to the Godhead for creating the heavens and the earth and all this universe contains. Thanks for reaching down and touching our lives in such a way, as revealed in these pages.

Next, I want to honor my wife Diana, and the covenant relationship God blessed us with. As we've had the opportunity to hold each other's hands through the changes and challenges of life, I can honestly say that she is the greatest witness to my life, apart from the Lord.

This book is dedicated to our children Niki, Nathan, Sharah, and Vanessa, their spouses, and our precious grandchildren. You mean the world to us!

I also want to take the opportunity to thank all the different pastors, teachers, Youth With A Mission leaders, students, staff, and friends I've gleaned from. I would list their names, but it would take pages to do so. So, thanks to all of you for your investment into the kingdom, and your influence in my life.

Finally, I want to thank the co-author of this book, William Dew. Every once in a while, we get a heaven-born relationship in life. Will has been one of those blessings.

Kip Gaines

CHAPTER 1

The Greater Miracle

What's the purpose of your life?

I used to think my purpose was to be a race car driver—a Formula One driver to be exact. I'm serious. I was dead set on racing in my teens and early twenties.

My obsession began after a string of traumatic experiences. When I was 13, my parents got divorced, our house burned down to the ground, and my dog (who was my best friend at the time) died in the fire. Then, to top it all off, my grandfather committed suicide. Thirteen was an incredibly painful year.

My mom started dating other men, and one of them took us to my first Formula One race. I was completely captivated. I can still remember the ground vibrating, as my ears filled with screaming 800 horsepower v12 engines flying by at 180 mph. I was hooked. More than an exciting race, I saw an opportunity. I saw a chance to be part of something bigger than myself. For the next decade, I was all in.

By my late teens, racing consumed all my thoughts, money, and time. I completed two high-performance driving schools, raced at a local track, and... totaled 15 cars. With both feet on the gas, I drew nearer to my purpose: becoming a Formula One driver, no matter what the cost.

But God had something greater in mind.

I always believed there was a God, but I never went to church. My first real experience with Christians was after my older sister and brother-in-law started following Jesus. Though I didn't receive their words, they kept praying for me and sharing their newfound hope. Soon afterward, God brought a woman into my life. I'll share in more detail later, but let's just say meeting Diana slowed my racing aspirations. Soon after we got married, she gave her life to Christ. Diana's love and encouragement drew me closer and closer to the Lord until I too surrendered my life.

I went *all in*.

To be honest, Kip Gaines is no one special. I don't have a Ph.D. or any major awards. I simply decided to go *all in* with Jesus. When you meet Him, get to know Him, and commit to walk with Him through the changes and challenges of life, He completely transforms you. He completely revolutionized my life and continues to transform me to this day.

Do you know God has a purpose for your life? Jeremiah 29:11 beautifully describes a life in the hands of a personal God:

> *For I know the plans I have for you, declares the LORD plans for welfare not for calamity for a future and a hope. Then you will call upon Me and find Me when you search for me with all your heart!*

God has a plan, a purpose for your life, and He'll share it if you search for Him with all your heart. *All* your heart. This *all* is much more than saying a prayer. It means you go *all in*. It means laying down your life, walking hand-in-hand with Jesus, and going wherever He leads. For me, *all in* meant selling my house, a successful business (Gaines Industries), and all my racing equipment. For my young family, it meant leaving our home, dreams, and our loved ones in Cleveland, Ohio to answer the call into full-time missions. And that was only the beginning.

Our family at Youth with a Mission, Tyler, TX (1991)

All in doesn't stop.

I know I see through a glass dimly and must continually bring my blunders to God, but my main desire is to keep holding His hand. That's my purpose. I'm *all in*. That means I honor God with my everyday decisions and hold on tight through times of conflict. It's not always easy, but through relational challenges, brain tumors, suicides, surviving terrorist attacks in Israel, health problems, and more, I just keep holding His hand.

The Bible calls this *shalom*.

Shalom

In the Bible, the Hebrew word *shalom* is usually translated as peace, but it's important to understand its root meaning. When most of us think of peace, we picture someplace quiet with sunshine, flowers, and everything in perfect harmony. That is not the Hebrew understanding.

The *Shalom* of God is not the absence of conflict. Rather, it's having authority over the conflicts of present-day life and discernment to destroy the source of chaos. Let me explain.

Ancient Hebrew began as a pictographic language—like Egyptian hieroglyphics. Their letters are not abstract, but symbols with meaning. For example, the Hebrew letter Lamed—ל—was originally a shepherd's crook. It makes an "L" sound, and it means authority.

Now let's look at the word *shalom*. (By the way, Hebrew writing goes right to left).

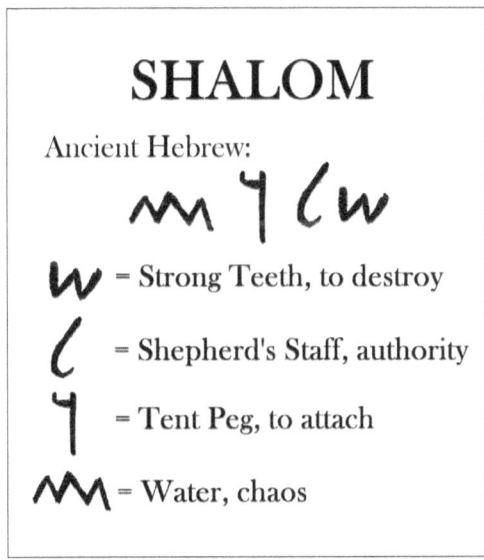

by Kip Gaines

According to the ancient letters, *shalom* literally means to destroy the authority attached to chaos. Though we live in a world of chaos, it should not have authority in our lives. Walking in *shalom*—the peace of God—means we view and respond to success, failure, and conflict so that chaos has no authority in our lives. When things are in the right order, we live in peace.

It's easy to blame our chaotic lives on other people and circumstances, but our peace is determined by our responses. We choose what to focus on, what has authority over our thoughts. It's only when we give authority to those lofty thoughts (that set themselves up against the knowledge of God), that our lives become out of order (chaotic). This book is designed to help you view life clearer, so even in a world of chaos, you can better walk in true *shalom*.

In this world, there will always be conflict. But conflict, when rightly responded to, is the surgical knife that strips us of our carnality and ushers us into the image of God. We can walk in *shalom* regardless of the conflicts we're facing.

At a conference several years ago, the speaker gave each of us a poster board and a stack of yellow Post-it Notes. He instructed us to write down our major life events on separate notes and arrange them in chronological order on the poster. After a few minutes, he handed out red Post-its and told us to mark all the major conflicts. Lastly, he gave us blue Post-it Notes to mark our greatest revelations of life-changing understanding or encounters with God. Can you picture it?

This book is designed to help you view life clearer, so even in a world of chaos, you can better walk in true shalom.

It was so eye-opening when we held up our poster boards, they all showed a similar pattern. Red Post-its were followed by blue ones. Revelatory prophetic impartations, times of healing, growth, and intimate connection with the Lord came right after some of our greatest conflicts.

Conflict rightly responded to positions us to receive greater revelation from the Lord. Brokenness often precedes the power of God in our lives. Responding rightly to hardship brings the *Shalom* of God into our lives.

We don't need to understand why. We don't need clarity. It's all about trust and holding tight onto God's hand. If you can't tell, I'm pretty passionate about this. This is not an abstract theological ideal, it's how we're called to live.

It's amazing how through God's grace, this *shalom* is possible in even the most difficult circumstances.

The Greater Miracle Vision

It happened in 1992, after my wife and I had been full-time missionaries with Youth With A Mission (YWAM) for nine years. We were busy with four kids and running Discipleship Training Schools, not to mention overseeing Base Prayer, the Worship Department, AV Department, working with a summer program for teens, and leading two foreign outreaches a year. Busy would be an understatement.

We were just about to kick off our next Discipleship Training School when, out of nowhere, Diana felt her equilibrium was off and everything sounded distant. She went home to rest, but by the next morning, she was much worse. When she woke up, she was totally paralyzed and very cold on her left side.

After being admitted to the hospital, and receiving a battery of MRI scans, the doctors found a brain malformation. My wife was diagnosed with a Cavernous Hemangioma Malformation in the pons of her brainstem. This particular type of tumor is usually harmless until it bleeds, which was the root of all her symptoms. And, according to the specialists, it would only be a matter of time before it bled again. The next bleed could be life-threatening. And unfortunately, because of its location, the surgery option was intolerable.

Diana was given six months to two years.

I was in a state of total shock and brokenness. The following days and weeks were a blur. I was overwhelmed and didn't know how to process it all. Everyone sounded like the adults in Charlie Brown. "Whah whah whah whaaah."

During one of my prayer times, the Lord gave me a vision. It began in a large auditorium filled with people. The elders brought a lady in a wheelchair down to the front. The lady was crippled with disease, and everyone began to pray. Then, all of a sudden, this woman was miraculously healed! She jumped up praising the Lord!

I said, "Oh my gosh, God! Are you going to heal my wife?"

Then something very peculiar occurred. The visions shifted to a globe. On the globe, I saw all the oceans splashing up onto the continents of the world. As the waves splashed further and further in, they became all sorts of people proclaiming the gospel of Jesus Christ, healing the sick, and setting people free.

For those of you who don't know, this is the same vision God gave YWAM's founder, Loren Cunningham. I remember telling God, "God, this is Loren's vision! This is the vision you gave him to start YWAM! God, why? Why are you giving me Loren's vision?"

Then the Lord asked me this question: "Son, what is the greater miracle? That I can raise a woman up out of a wheelchair and heal her physical body? Or that tens of thousands of my sons and daughters make the free will choice to surrender their lives to Me, being a witness of my life, giving their lives to the nations of the world, fulfilling the Great Commission?"

Wow. I answered, "The tens of thousands of your sons and daughters making the free will choice to surrender their lives and fulfilling the Great Commission!"

The Lord said, "That's correct! *You* are the greater miracle."

Let me tell you something. If you love Jesus and you made the free will choice to surrender your will to Him, then God says you are the greater miracle!

If you go *all in* with Jesus, you are the greater miracle. You are the greater miracle!

Do you realize the magnitude of what you are part of? This thing we call the body of Christ is not something to be taken lightly. In fact, 2 Corinthians declares you as a Bible character of today!

> *You are our letter, written in our hearts, known and read by all*
> *men; being manifested that you are a letter of Christ, written not*
> *with ink but with the Spirit of the living God, not on tablets of stone*
> *but on tablets of human hearts* (2 Cor. 3:2-3).

Like Paul's letters, which became scripture, our lives should also declare the truth and power of the gospel. Biblical truth is not about an intellectual assessment of facts but knowing a person. His name is Jesus Christ—the way, the truth, and the life (John 14:6). He gives your life purpose.

Life is all about relationship. When we take the risk, lay down our lives, go *all in*, then our only option is to hold God's hand through the changes and challenges of life. That's what it means to trust God! It's not just saying you have faith but living like those mentioned in Hebrews 11. When we truly trust, God calls us His child and we get to know Him in ways we never thought possible.

You are the greater miracle.

This book is not about teaching impersonal facts. I want you to have a better relationship with the Truth. The revelations and experiences in the following pages are the result of much prayer, fasting, study, seeking the Lord, and holding His hand. I'm not sharing these as just a set of teachings but as an extension of my relationship with God. These core foundational principles are my understanding of the Biblical Worldview. It's the foundation I've built my life upon and how I've encouraged thousands to live in greater intimacy with an extravagant God.

With the correct perception of reality, the Biblical Worldview, we live abundant lives with purpose. This proper foundation provides a framework of understanding to better interpret the world around us and continually live in *shalom*. And when the storms of life hit, we can stand firm on the Truth, trusting the One who loves us most.

Don't just read these words. Take an honest look at how you view the world and allow the Truth to bring loving correction. Let's walk this journey together, and honor God with each and every decision that we make. As my friend Dean Sherman says, "Everything God does, He has us in mind. All He asks is that everything we do, we have Him in mind." I want you to grab a hold of His hand and never let go no matter what. If you do, you are the greater miracle.

Oh God, give me shalom. I want to walk in your peace and hold your hand through the changes and challenges of life. Everything I do, I want to have you in mind! Reveal yourself to me in a greater way. Use this book to increase my wisdom and cause me to walk closer with you.

———

Download your free *Discussion/Study Guide* for group and individual discipleship. Visit www.kipgaines.com/allin

CHAPTER 2

Who Do You Say that I Am? (Framework)

Biblical concepts can get complicated. Back in Jesus' day, the religious leaders not only followed the law but additional traditions that made things way more complicated. I like what Jesus did. He summed up the law and the prophets. He didn't get caught up in the details but revealed God's heart to clear up the details.

In the same way, concepts like worldview and God's nature can easily get complex. My desire is to get to the heart of the matter. Using scripture, I want to break concepts down to their most basic form to lay out clear foundational principles. I find that going to the most basic form of Biblical concepts helps me to systematically understand and apply the Word to my life. That way, many details, disagreements, and questions get cleared up.

It's like one of those 3D Magic Eye pictures. You know what I'm talking about? It just looks like an ugly mess of dots and stuff. The first time I saw one, I didn't get it. I tried to go cross-eyed or whatever, but I couldn't see a thing. I thought it was some kind of joke.

Then, all of a sudden, my eyes refocused and, "WOAH! Check it out! There's a dolphin! I can totally see it!"

A picture was there all along, but I didn't have the eyes to see it. When we don't have the correct perspective, the image is hidden, and the picture looks like a random mess. But when we learn how to look at these images the right way, we can easily see the true picture. It's the same with our worldview.

Our worldview is the lens, or perspective, we see the world through. It determines how we answer the BIG questions in life. Who am I? Who is God? What's my purpose? etc. Even if we never take the time to fully articulate our beliefs, these questions are answered by the choices we make every day.

To live in peace, in God's *shalom*, we must understand what we believe.

We cannot have a concept of God we are unable or unwilling to live up to without it causing agitation to our souls. Likewise, we cannot have a concept of ourselves we are unable or unwilling to live up to without a similar agitation. This is why so many of us are somewhat agitated!

Take, for example, the foundational Biblical concept of being saved, or what Jesus referred to as being born again. What does that mean? In the Sermon on the Mount (Matt. 5-7), Jesus teaches sinners: "be pure in heart," "turn the other cheek," "be fully devoted to God," and many other difficult commands. Jesus set a standard no one could meet on their own. In this famous sermon, He made it clear we need more than just a teacher. We need a Savior! We need a Savior to prepare us to receive His teachings (truth) and develop a correct worldview. So, when we ask Jesus, "Who am I?" He gets to the heart of the answer by asking, "Who do you say that I am?"

We can never truly be saved until we receive the Savior personally. The Church is made up of those who know His identity, Jesus as *the Messiah*. That's me! Jesus is my Savior! I know Jesus like Peter did (Matt. 16): "You are the Christ, the Son of the Living God."

How about you? Do you know Jesus as just a teacher or is He your Savior?

When Peter fully understood who Jesus is, Jesus spoke to his identity. Jesus changed Simon's name to Peter, from "he who hears" (Simon) to "rock" (Peter). Our identity does not rest on us discovering who we are. Our identity rests on the discovery of who He is.

If we believe the Bible is true, we must accept the worldview it presents to be the correct perception of reality—the Biblical Worldview. This perspective doesn't come naturally, but supernaturally after we meet Jesus and commit to holding His hand. He not only gives our lives value and purpose but also invites us into a whole new stratosphere of understanding. This must transform how we see the world.

Our identity does not rest on us discovering who we are.
Our identity rests on the discovery of who He is.

If we want to be like Jesus, we must see the world from His point of view—the Biblical Worldview. As we allow Him to refocus our (world)view, just like those 3D Magic Eye pictures, specific concepts and world events make more sense.

Now, there's no specific book or chapter in the Bible that spells out a full Biblical worldview. However, God invites us to seek, study, and (with the help of the Holy Spirit) find the knowledge of the Truth (1 Tim. 2:4). But let me warn you, if you get too focused on specific aspects of this worldview, things can quickly become complex and confusing. Theologians have studied and debated specific facets for centuries. Remember, going to the most basic form of Biblical concepts helps us to systematically understand and apply the Word to our lives.

The Framework

It's important to outline a simple framework, a clear foundation to build on. Through walking with God and studying His word, I've found consistent principles laid out in the Bible. These principles serve as guides to process life, understand God's will, and hold His hand through it all. They answer those BIG questions, providing a framework to better understand the Bible and the world around us. They also provide a firm foundation to build our beliefs upon. Once we establish a foundation, we can then enjoy a lifestyle of fellowship that can stand the test of time.

First, I'll lay out the overall framework and then explain.

We live in a world of:

One Gods—Father, Son, and Holy Spirit

Five Influences—God, the adversary, ourselves, others, and circumstance

Three Heavens—physical realm, the spiritual realm, and the Highest Heaven

Three Origins of Thought—us, God, and the adversary

Two Kingdoms—the Kingdom of God and the Kingdom of the adversary

As we examine these concepts, you'll see they're surprisingly basic—which makes them that much more important. These concepts are not fabricated by man. They are simply laid out clearly in the Bible. I believe God helped me articulate this systematic approach to present foundational truths in an applicable way. If you understand this framework, you'll better understand why things happen.

Three Heavens and Five Influences

For example, let's unpack the concept of three heavens and five influences. In the Bible, three heavens, or realms, are mentioned.

1. The first heaven is the physical realm in which we live. It's the world God created, the physical world we can see and interact with using our senses.

2. The second heaven is the spiritual realm mentioned in Revelations 12, Daniel 10, and elsewhere. This realm is where Satan and the other rebellious angels were cast and where they fight the angels of light. From this realm, powers and principalities influence the physical world through accusation, deception, etc. This heavenly realm is where our battle must be fought according to Ephesians 6:12.

3. Then there's the third heaven, which most of us regard as THE Heaven. This is the realm where God dwells in His glory. It is perfect and no evil dwells there. It's not clouds and naked baby angels with harps (that's not in the Bible), but a realm where God's will is perfectly done. Paul talks about his experience in this third heaven in 2 Corinthians 12 and John describes it in his revelation (Revelations).

So, there are the three heavens. Got it?

Now let's move on to the five influences. We don't have to do an in-depth Bible study to recognize there are different influences at work in this world. When God created beings (angels and humans) with the ability to choose (free will), five influences were a natural result. I know there are many different views in Christianity about how much of life is predestined or not, but let's not get caught up in that. Specific doctrines aside, the Bible reveals five influences that cause events to happen as they do:

1. God's influence

2. The adversary's influence

3. Our own choices

4. Other people's choices

5. Circumstance

First, I'll address the spiritual influences. Foremost, there is a loving God who made covenant with His creation. He maintains order in the universe; "by His hand, all things hold together" (Col. 1:16). Thank God He holds us together. Ultimately, His will, will be done. But in His wisdom and love, He allows others to exert their influence also.

Secondly, there is an adversary out there who also has a plan for your life. "The thief comes to steal, kill, and destroy" (John 10:10). Satan and his forces operate in the second heaven, exerting their influence against the purposes of God.

"Not all is well with the world. War has come to God's world. War that began long ago in heaven and will not cease until the Prince of Peace takes back what is rightfully His."
—Winkie Pratney

You may be wondering why I keep saying "the adversary" instead of the Devil or Satan. There is an important truth here. Many Christians esteem Satan too highly. Yes, there is a Lucifer, who was a powerful angel who led the rebellion against God (Isa. 14, Ex. 28). But when you go back to the original language, you find something interesting. Satan, in Hebrew, is always *ha satan* which literally means *the adversary*. In the New Testament, the devil is not necessarily a specific being, but rather Greek for *the adversary*. Of course, we need to be aware of the existence and influence of our adversaries or enemies. But when the Bible mentions Satan or the devil, it could mean Lucifer or any other spirit adverse to the Spirit of God. And regardless of whether we're talking about Lucifer or all the adversaries combined, neither is a match for our God!

In the past, I included a separate influence here: angelic influence. Though angels do have free will, their influence is either fully submitted securing God's will or not. The Bible suggests that those lines have been drawn, so for simplicity's sake, angelic influence is included in either God's or the adversary's influence. We'll look at this in a later chapter.

The next two influences, our choices and others' choices, are both a result of human free will. Just as we exert our influence, so does every other person on this planet. These influences are simply the results of the decisions we make every day. God's will is perfect, and aligning our influence with His increases the chance it will be accomplished.

Unfortunately, God's perfect will is not always realized as different influences tend to clash. This brings the final influence into play, which is the clashing of influences—or circumstance. Jesus confirms this influence in Luke 13:1-5. He talks about people who died, not because of their wickedness, but the unfortunate circumstance of a falling tower. Obviously, circumstance (or the clash of influences) can have profound effects.

In this world of three heavens, these five influences are always at work. Before you are saved, after you're saved, even in the process of you committing yourself to Jesus, these five influences are present. Though we can choose to believe in the existence of three heavens and five influences, our choice does not change the way the world works. We must accept that the temporal dovetails into that which is eternal. We will only understand reality when we align our perspective with the Biblical worldview.

Lord Jesus, help me to see the world the way it truly is. Establish the Biblical Worldview, the correct perception of reality, in my heart and mind. Holy Spirit, help me establish a firm foundation to build my life upon and fix any aspects that aren't correctly aligned. Help me to align my influence and my will, with yours. I want to know you and understand who I am in you. Only then, can I stand firm even when other influences cause confusion and pain. Jesus, establish me on you, the Truth.

Download your free *Discussion/Study Guide* for group and individual discipleship. Visit www.kipgaines.com/allin

CHAPTER 3

The Importance of Listening (Guidance)

How did you get saved?

When I was 26, I heard a message on the cross and went up to the altar weeping. I felt an overwhelming love that I didn't fully understand but demanded my response. I knew God had a plan for my life and I said, "Yes." I can still hear the song "Just As I Am" playing. So impacted by this unconditional love and acceptance, Diana and I sold our house, our business, and immediately moved across the country to serve God as missionaries.

During my YWAM training (School of the Bible to be exact), I wrote a paper on the conditions of salvation and learned something amazing. Through my study, I discovered the first condition of salvation. Do you know what it is? It's neither faith nor repentance. The first condition of salvation is *listening*, hearing God's voice. "Faith comes by hearing and hearing by the Word of God" (Rom. 10:17).

We see this in both the New and Old Testaments.

"If you harken unto the voice of the Lord and diligently obey all His commands..." (Deut. 28:1-2).

"Jesus said: My sheep hear my voice then obey my word" (John 10).

We must first listen and then obey.

The Lord loves us unconditionally—while we were yet sinners (Rom. 5:8)! He speaks first. He knocks first. He reaches out first. He searches first. He reveals the need for forgiveness to walk in relationship. Salvation is a gift of God!

Listening is so important. It puts us in the correct posture of receiving and provides an opportunity to trust Him. We cannot earn salvation, love, purpose, provision, or even self-acceptance. But if we are in a posture of listening, then we can receive these as gifts. It's called rest. God declares this as righteousness (Heb. 11).

Do you know what brings more joy to the heart of God than anything else described in the Bible from creation to Revelation? When His children overcome this environment of pain, suffering, and uncertainty and emerge trusting Him.

God, I trust you!

We were created for relationship with our Creator. Whenever we seek the Lord for guidance our main motivation then must be: "Lord, where would I be most intimate with You?" When this is our chief desire, it puts a smile on His heart and—you mark my words—He will bless!

Difficulties Concerning Guidance

When seeking God for guidance we must realize that the call of God on our lives is relational, not geographical or for a task. When God calls us to a nation or to a task, take note. Don't be disappointed by unmet expectations. Success is having intimacy with God and those we're privileged to partner with! Our journey isn't just to reach a particular end, but to walk in the continual word of the Lord.

Toward the end of my School of the Bible training, I was presented with ten different vocational opportunities. I wanted to make the best decision for the Lord and my family, so I did a 40-day fast (of water and some bread) to devote myself to the Lord. During that time, my main prayer was: "GOD! I need to know the word of the Lord. I need to know what You want me to do. What's best for my family?"

One night, as I was crying out, He spoke to me very clearly and said, "No, Kip. You don't need the word of the Lord. You need to walk in a present tense intimacy with Me. This is key in knowing how to get the word of the Lord."

Wow. Did you hear that? Yes, that word was given to me, but I believe this is God's heart for each of His children. We don't need clarity; we need to soak up the journey. Walking intimately with the Lord is paramount. God doesn't want to simply give us a one-time word, but principles to apply in all situations.

As we walk and listen, it's important to understand how God speaks. In the New Testament, there are two different kinds of words. There is the *logos* word, which is the written word (Bible) and then there is the *rayma* word, which is a specific word for the moment. Now, obviously, knowing God's word is extremely important, and in the Bible, God teaches us how to hear his voice. Does it make sense to teach us how to hear then stop speaking? Of course not! He longs to give us fresh manna—our DAILY bread.

Unfortunately, some believers try to only live on one type of word or the other. They seek only the *logos* or only the *rayma*. Both these words are important and need to be balanced. To just know the written word, does not make you a person of truth. The Pharisees are great examples of people obeying the letter of the law but missing the *rayma* completely. To only walk in the *rayma*, does not make you a person of truth. Remember, we live in a world of five influences and three heavens that are always at work. You must make sure that the *rayma* you receive is confirmed by the *logos*.

Let me put it another way. As we understand the *logos* (by studying the Bible) we learn who God is and His guiding principles. God will not contradict Himself. However, we can't live by principles alone because that's not the whole truth. The Truth is a person, and His name is Jesus. We also need to walk in the *rayma* to know how to apply the *logos*. There is nothing in the Bible that says whether you should or shouldn't be a politician or a pastor. Biblical principles examine our hearts to test our motives, while the *rayma* word works in concert giving us direction for now.

This brings us to the primary issue. Many questions of guidance can be resolved by simply checking our motives. We want to know an answer, but God wants us to know Him in truth and grace. Once we get on the same page and agree with His objective, things become clear. More than merely doing the right thing, God cares about the motivation of your heart.

Whenever you seek God on anything, if the motive or intention of your heart is intimacy with Jesus, then you can't go wrong. God is really big, loving, and powerful. Even if your decision wasn't His best, if you're truly motivated by faith, He can make it into your best. It's this relational dynamic that determines the success of our guidance. Trusting God when taking risks is how we get to see God as our deliverer! He loves that!

The 5 Steps of Guidance

If our motives are pure and we desire God's will to be done, we can move forward with the principles of guidance. In the Bible, there are five different steps that help us discern God's voice. None of the steps are guidance by themselves, only 1/5th of guidance.

- 1/5 guidance: Scripture; a passage that stands out
- 1/5 guidance: A Still Small Voice; peace or check
- 1/5 guidance: Wise Council; both natural and spiritual

- 1/5 guidance: Providential Circumstances
- 1/5 guidance: Prophetic Words; confirmation only

Because of this world of five influences and three heavens, it's wise to not rely on our interpretation of one step alone. However, if three steps line up and our motives are correct, it's probably God. If all five areas line up, I'd call that a miracle. Usually, God wants us to step out in faith with partial guidance. This risk of trusting God brings Him much pleasure. To those who step out, He declares, "I am their God" (Heb. 11).

Now let's look at each one of these in more detail.

1. Scriptures that leap off the page

There are times when we study and a particular passage jumps out. Isn't the Bible amazing?! It's the Living Word!

Even familiar scriptures can stand out in a new way. When this happens, it's important to faithfully record these verses, even if they seem unrelated or the reason isn't apparent. Remember, God rewards those who diligently seek Him (Heb. 11:6). Many times, He'll weave a thread through different verses and reveal something incredible about Himself. But remember, scripture is always true, scripture may *not* be specific guidance. Scriptures are 1/5 of guidance. Let me tell you a story from my experience as the director of DTS:

Many years ago, we had an exceptionally encouraging young man as a student. One evening, a female student visited our home and told us she had a list of scriptures confirming the man she was going to marry—this particular encouraging young man.

A few days later, a different girl came into my office and shared a list of scriptures pointing to her future husband. Guess what? It was the same guy. In fact, by the end of that school, five different girls had lists of scriptures confirming they were going to marry this guy. And, as you've probably guessed, he ended up marrying someone else. Our hearts can deceive us. Our interpretation of scripture is not guidance. Scriptures that leap off the page are 1/5 of guidance.

2. A Still Small Voice

If you are saved, you know His voice. That still small voice can come in many ways, but often it's recognized as a peace or a check. Your spirit just knows that something feels right or wrong. This is different than an irrational fear or rationalizing. And again, this isn't guidance by itself.

If I allowed every check in my spirit to stop me, I'd probably never do anything for God. The enemy, my own fears and insecurities, or someone else can speak doubt which can be interpreted as a check. Other times, that check is God's protection.

Most often, this still small voice confirms the other steps of guidance. It's important not to allow a single step, or 1/5 of guidance, to set our expectations. This can cause unnecessary confusion.

One morning, when my wife and I were living in the jungles of southern Belize, I was in an outhouse. All of a sudden, I felt the presence of the Lord really thick. His still small voice said, "You will have a son and his name will be Jacob Grandison Gaines."

Discipleship at Eagles Nest Punta Gorda, Belize (1989)

My wife wasn't pregnant, but when we talked about it, she mentioned recording six different scriptures about Jacob in her journal. It seemed as if God was confirming His word. We were expectant. I even took a picture in front of the outhouse and excitedly shared the story with all of our supporters in our next newsletter. Months later, Diana conceived, and we traveled back to the United States. Before we knew it, we had a perfect, healthy baby *girl*. I was overjoyed, but I was also in shock.

I was convinced I heard Jacob from the Lord. Did I miss God? This Jacob thing became a point of shame, and I tried to forget about it.

Years later, while we were leading a Discipleship Training School, some incredible young men stopped by our house. These students were seeking the Lord together and kept getting scriptures about Jacob. They then shared six different scriptures and asked if we had any more understanding.

The most incredible thing happened. Diana quickly dug out her old journal from our time in Belize. The six scriptures they shared weren't just the same on her journal, but the scriptures were in the same order!

I went before the Lord. "God!? What does this mean?"

The Lord made it very clear that I didn't miss Him. Then He put the pieces together:

- *Jacob* represents ISRAEL, His sons and daughters

- *Grandison* was Charles Finney's middle name, representing the systematic theology I teach

- *Gaines* represents that they are my disciples

The Lord then shared, "This is the reason I allowed you to go through the painful process of thinking that you missed Me and the shame of miscommunicating. I am imparting something to you that will be a part of who you are for the rest of your life. When I entrust you with souls to disciple, treat them as if they were your own kids because they are My sons and daughters.

As you're running training schools, mentoring young leaders, I want you to know that first and foremost they're My kids and My children are precious in my sight. No matter what they are dealing with, or how challenging they are, I want you to treat them as if they were your own flesh and blood children."

I fell down and wept.

Since then, I have never wavered from this impartation God gave me. I treat each one I have the blessing of discipling as my own child. Scriptures confirmed this word miraculously and solidified His still small voice. Remember, there are five influences at work and peace is only 1/5th of guidance.

3. Wise Counsel

There are many verses about the importance of wise counsel when making decisions (Prov. 11:14, 12:15, 15:22, etc.). Now there are two forms of wise counsel that need to be considered here, which are both important. First, there is natural counsel from people knowledgeable in certain areas. This counsel is practical, from a natural perspective, with concerns for health, well-being, finances, etc. Second, there is spiritual counsel from someone you trust with spiritual maturity and who wants you to have intimacy with Jesus. In both cases, it's smart to consider the counselor's relationship with you and the situation. Knowledge of your history or gifting can be beneficial. On the other hand, even well-meaning advisors may not be the best counsel if they are directly impacted by the decision. Remember there are five influences at work.

Wise counsel alone is not guidance, it's 1/5th. The only unadulterated word of God comes directly from God. God does speak through people, but remember, that word is then processed through our worldview, gifting, relationships, and attitudes. Seek both natural and spiritual council. I recommend someone knowledgeable of the situation and someone trustworthy with no vested interest. And of course, weigh your counsel with the other steps of guidance.

4. Providential Circumstances

Sometimes events point in a specific direction. If we pray for a job and one opens up, that's a good indicator. However, in this world of five influences and three heavens, we should hold all things with an open hand. Even if something seems *perfect* for us, our Heavenly Father is really smart. He knows us better than we know ourselves (Ps. 139). Circumstances alone are not guidance.

5. The Prophetic

These are supernatural events, visions, dreams, prophetic words, visitations, etc. In the Bible, God spoke through angelic visitations, signs, and wonders. Now, some of you may be quoting, "It's a wicked and perverse generation that seeks a sign" (Matt. 12:39). We will discuss this in more detail later, but this verse has everything to do with motivation. The religious leaders didn't acknowledge the miracles Jesus did or have relationship with Him but would only believe if God met them on their terms. If you are holding God's hand and relating to Him, it's ok to ask for a sign. This is not to test the Lord; we are supposed to seek Him not just His hand. But remember, prophetic words are not meant to be our only source of guidance. The prophetic should confirm the other steps.

Again, each of these steps is 1/5th of guidance. If our motives are pure and three of these five steps point the same way, it's probably the Holy Spirit's leading. Step out in faith, trusting the Good Shepard will continue to guide you. Your Father is loving, and if He is leading, it's the best and you can rest.

There are times when God doesn't answer our specific questions, but He speaks. If you are saved, He is speaking to you. We may prefer a clear yes or no, but more often God changes our mindsets and attitudes. He's not concerned with tasks as much as conforming us into His image. When we obediently step out to follow Him, then He releases more of the answer (Luke 16:10).

> *None of the steps are guidance by themselves,*
> *only 1/5th of guidance.*

When my wife Diana and I seek guidance for a big decision, we buy a little notebook and mark a tab for each step. Writing down our process is incredibly helpful in so many ways. There have been other times, like the Jacob Grandison Gaines story, when we experienced an unexpected outcome. Sometimes we're not sure if we heard God correctly. Being able to go back and review the five steps brings so much peace in times of questioning.

And remember, if God is silent, He's not the problem. Even though many saints experience a season where God doesn't speak, in retrospect, the silence has purpose and can communicate deeper than words. Silence also realigns our motives and helps us see the actual questions we should ask.

Finally, our main goal should not be an answer, but the adventure of walking with God and learning how to hear His voice. As we seek Him and step out in faith, we will grow in deeper intimacy with God. Guidance is not a burden, it's a blessing. To hear the voice of God and follow is one of the greatest privileges of believers. It's a manifestation of our relationship with God. If you are seeking intimacy with Jesus as you seek guidance, you will hear things from God that will blow you away.

The coolest thing about being in a relationship with God is He wants relationship; He wants our hearts. As we seek the Lord and walk out in obedience, He is most excited about walking on this journey with you—His son or daughter.

Father, this is it! I'm going all in. I trust you. Let your Kingdom come and will be done in me. Holy Spirit, give me shalom when hearing your voice. I want to recognize and remove any authority causing chaos in my thoughts. Grant me the gift to recognize accusation and deception clouding my vision. Give me ears to hear and eyes to see. Help me tune into the Good Shepherd's voice in the midst of distractions. More than simply getting answers to questions, purify my motives and help me embrace the process. Give me discernment to hear your voice, boldness to step out in faith, and lead me to where I'll have the most intimacy with you.

CHAPTER 4

What Does *All In* Really Look Like (Ultimate Intent)

In case you somehow missed it in the last chapter, our motives are really, really, really important. While religion focuses on doing right things, God cares more about being in right relationship. Jesus shared this truth over and over again, especially when being questioned by the religious leaders.

> *Jesus gave them this answer: "I tell you the truth, the Son can do nothing by himself; he can do only what he sees his Father doing, because whatever the Father does the Son also does." (John 5:19)*

Jesus was *all in*. When He walked the earth, He showed us the simplicity of being *all in*. He simply did what He saw His Father doing. This was (and still is) the ultimate intention of Jesus' heart, so the Father empowered Jesus to accomplish His will.

When we go *all in*, the same should be said of us.

But take a moment here and be honest: What's the ultimate intention of your heart? I'm talking about your reason for living, your motivation, the bottom-line purpose of your life. The ultimate intention of your heart is why you do what you do.

We make tons of choices every day. Sometimes, our ultimate intent is obvious. Big choices can lead us to clear consequences, but don't discount the importance of our *small* decisions.

All choices have consequences. Most choices are subordinate. These are the small, supporting decisions, that are made every day with little or no thought. Things like eating, going to the bathroom, and clipping toenails may seem insignificant, but why we do them is extremely significant.

When I teach our high school summer programs, I use a specific illustration to capture this point (and the student's attention). Humor can be the best way to make a lasting impression.

Anyway, before drawing these two cartoons, I let the class know the first character is a sinner and the second is righteous. As I draw, they are supposed to guess what the characters are doing. Now, my wife is an artist, I was a race car driver. This chalkboard drawing is no masterpiece, but it doesn't take long for kids to start guessing.

"He's... DRIVING A CAR!"

"SOMEONE SITTING DOWN!"

"A BOY WAITING FOR SOMEONE?!"

"Noooooo... I KNOW! I KNOW! THEY'RE ON THE TOILET!!!"

Now, I don't want to offend anyone, but these cartoon characters make an important point. Stick with me. (These are my real drawings by the way.)

by Kip Gaines

When the comments and laughter die down, I ask, "Why? Why are these guys going to the bathroom?" Students yell out different reasons:

"Because they have to!" "To keep from getting sick!" "So they don't explode!" "God made them that way!"

Then I ask, "Is it sinful to go poop? Or is it righteous go poop?"

The class laughs again and argues a bit. They usually conclude neither. These two are just going poop.

I disagree. I believe it is a sinful subordinate choice when a sinner decides to go poop. I believe it is a righteous lifestyle decision of worship when a saint serves God by deciding to go to the bathroom.

The reason a righteous person goes to the bathroom is so that he can remain healthy. If the ultimate intention of his heart is to love and serve

God, going to the bathroom supports that ultimate intent. He goes to the bathroom, so he can remain healthy, so he can do more righteousness, building the kingdom of God.

The reason a sinner goes to the bathroom is also to remain healthy, but the ultimate intention of his heart is different. Because the ultimate intent of his heart is selfishness, then he goes to the bathroom so he can remain healthy, so he can continue his lifestyle of selfishness. For him, going to the bathroom is a sin.

Subordinate choices may seem innocent; however, they reveal our true motivation. These small decisions are the foundation that supports the ultimate intention of our hearts. When we realize this truth, we can enjoy doing the most mundane things as we keep God in mind in all that we do.

"Whether you eat or drink or whatever you do, do all to the glory of God" (1 Cor. 10:27).

If Jesus is Lord of your life, the ultimate intention of your heart is to do with your stuff what Jesus did with His stuff. All our choices, big or subordinate, are motivated by the intentions of our heart, build a kingdom, secure an end, and ultimately determine our destiny.

Have you ever said: "Why the heck did I do that?" or "What am I doing?" or "What's wrong with me?" I know I have. Why do we say such things? Sometimes, it's because our subordinate choices are left unchecked by either ignorance of the Word of God or a lack of the presence of God in our life. We are not even aware of the origin of our thoughts or the purpose for which we live our lives.

Too often, we make decisions only based on the temporal consequences. We don't see, or we don't consider, the ultimate end. The Proverbs remind us that "there is a way that seems right to a man," (Prov. 14:12) but that way can have unforeseen consequences.

Leaving the father's house seemed right to the prodigal son (Luke 15). It seemed like life would be better living life his own way. No doubt life was pleasurable for a short period, but his choices ultimately led him to deception (and eating pig slop). For us, living life our own way may bring some temporal pleasures, but it comes at a cost. Where are your choices leading you?

Some argue that they can love outside of God's created design. Maybe they believe the ultimate intention of their heart is to love people or some other good motivation. The Bible is clear that "God tests the heart" (Prov. 17:3, 2 Chron. 6:30) but it's also clear that we can't do things our own way (rich young ruler of Mark 10, Prov. 14:12). If we are honest, when our motivation is based on our own good intentions, things easily end up like Black Beauty.

Black Beauty

Have you ever heard this classic story? I know it's a book, but I saw the movie. It powerfully illustrates the danger of good intentions with a lack of knowledge. I'll set the scene...

The star of the show is a horse named Black Beauty. The other main character is a little boy, Joe, whose family owns Black Beauty. Joe LOVES Black Beauty. Joe wants to be around Black Beauty every chance he gets, but he's too young to take care of Beauty. There's also a hired stable hand who knows all about horses and he takes good care of Black Beauty while the little boy watches.

One day, Joe's mom begins hemorrhaging and is on the verge of bleeding to death. The stable hand jumps on Black Beauty and races across the town to get the doctor. When the doctor hears the dire news, he wants to help, but his son took their horse to town. If they wait for his son's return the mom could bleed to death. The stable hand looks at Black Beauty, who is panting from the trip, but he knows Beauty is special.

"Beauty will do it," he declares.

So, the doctor hops on and Black Beauty gallops back to the house.

Luckily, the doctor arrives in time to save the mom, but Beauty almost collapses from exhaustion. The stable hand is back at the doctors' house, so he can't take care of the horse. But Joe LOVES Black Beauty! Joe decides to take care of his horse, so he slowly leads Black Beauty to the stable for some ice water.

If you've seen the movie, or know anything about horses, you know this is a terrible idea. If you give hot, sweaty horses ice-cold water, it shocks their systems. The extreme temperature change can cause colic—even death.

Beauty is on the verge of death when the stable hand returns. He realizes the problem and quickly warms Black Beauty's stomach. Luckily, Beauty is saved, but without that intervention, Joe would've killed Black Beauty.

Can you believe it? Why would Joe do that? Joe LOVES Black Beauty, right? But he almost KILLED Black Beauty! Joe thought ice-cold water was the highest good for Black Beauty, but it wasn't. I'll finish with stable hand's powerful statement: "I don't know what causes more pain and suffering on the face of this earth—whether it's ignorance or wickedness of heart."

Being ignorant is dangerous. We've all had Black Beauty experiences when we tried to help someone or fix a situation, but just ended up making things worse. Unfortunately, a knowledgeable stable hand isn't always around to save the day.

We are so frail, living in this first heaven with a limited perspective and dealing with multiple influences. How can we possibly live this life rightly and really love others? It's too big for us to do alone. Thankfully, God never intended you to do it on your own. He designed this life to be all about relationship, that we would live our lives holding His hand.

The reality is, if you say you love but you don't submit yourself to God, you are either deceived or lying. At best, you love in ignorance and can cause a lot of damage. Joe LOVED Black Beauty, but his best intentions almost destroyed the very one he loved.

To say you love and yet reject the most loving, intelligent being in the universe, is to be blinded by pride. If we are open, we will hear God say, "Arise, oh sleeper, and come to your senses!"

It is Time to go All In

I'm sure you've heard the popular parable of the Prodigal Son. (Read Luke 15 if you need a quick refresher.) It's an incredible picture of God's heart, but I want to fast forward to one scene toward the end. The son disrespects his father, leaves the house, squanders his inheritance, and then a famine hits. He's in a far country with nothing and no one. The only job he finds is feeding pigs, and as you can imagine that doesn't pay too well. He eventually becomes so hungry, his mouth waters for the slop he's feeding pigs. Have you ever seen what pigs eat? Talk about hitting rock bottom.

One day, the young man "came to his senses" (v.17). Now, what does that "came to his senses" mean? Was he knocked out, needing smelling salts to revive consciousness? Had he fainted from hunger? No. He was fully conscious, but he was in what is called a stupor. He was in a state of making mindless choices, ones based in rote, and unaware (or unconscious) of their consequences. He made a lot of choices, big and small, that brought him to a place of wanting to eat pig slop.

Just like the Prodigal "came to his senses" and decided to go back home, we must come to our senses and allow our love for Jesus to motivate our decisions. We must trust God, hold His hand through the changes and challenges of life, and do what we see Him doing!

While reading this chapter, maybe you've realized the same thing I've realized. There's been a few times where I thought was *all in*, trying to do good things, but God revealed my true motivation. If this is happening to you, don't stop doing the good! You only need to change the ultimate intention of your heart. *All In* simply means everything we do, we have Him in mind. It means we process our decisions through our relationship with Him, not just intellectually right choices. It means returning to our first love, giving Jesus preeminence.

When we do stuff with God, no matter how small, the power of heaven causes it to bear fruit. This is why we can rejoice in even the mundane, repetitive tasks knowing they produce Christ in us and others. To live is Christ, to die is gain (Phil. 1:21)! It is not I who lives but Christ in me (Gal. 2:20)! When this is our motivation, then with Christ we can say: I only do what I see the Father doing (John 5:19).

This same sentiment is echoed in Revelation 2, where Jesus gives John a message for the church in Ephesus. He begins, "I know your deeds, your hard work, your perseverance..." He recognized the Ephesians' efforts and endurance, but then He challenges their motivation. He then challenges them to "remember [their] first love" (Rev. 2:4), the ultimate intention of their heart.

The only way to ensure your subordinate choices are lined up with God's will is to continually set Him as the ultimate intention of your heart. When your motives are in right order then your tree can start bearing good fruit that will last (John 15:16). You don't even need the law if the ultimate intention of your heart is to love God. "A good tree does not bring forth bad fruit, and a bad tree does not bring forth good fruit" (Matt. 7:18). Galatians says there is no law against the fruit of the spirit (5:22). If you love God and the ultimate intent of your heart is to glorify Him with your life, of course you won't kill or steal. The reason I'm faithful to my wife is not because it's one of the Ten Commandments. I'm faithful because I love her. If you love God, and really trust in His goodness, you won't covet or walk in pride thinking your will is more important.

And there's more good news. If our hearts are right, we don't have to fear ignorance. God can correct our mistakes and will listen even if we pray uneducated prayers. There's a story in the book of Joshua (10) where Joshua prays a really stupid prayer. He and the Israelites are fighting for their Promise Land as the Lord commanded them. But the battle lasts all day, and the sun starts going down. Joshua prays, "Sun, stand still!"

Umm... Ok, Joshua... the sun is always still. What a stupid prayer, right?

Though he prayed in ignorance, the Lord still honored it. He knew Joshua's heart and it was in accordance with His will. God answered Joshua's uneducated prayer:

"And the sun stood still, and the moon stayed, until the nation had avenged themselves on their enemies" (v. 13).

If we pray the wrong thing with the right heart motive, God will look at your heart and not the accuracy of your perception. He understands your limitations. He looks at a man's heart, not his brain. Yes, He wants us to gain understanding and be wise (Prov. 3:13, 4:1, basically the whole book), but we'll never have all knowledge. We can, however, make sure our motivation is correct.

Of course, we can then ask, what really is our motivation? We don't even know our own hearts, right? Our "heart is deceitful…, who can know it?" (Jer. 17:9). But guess what? If you are unsure of your heart's ultimate intention, you can ask God. Hebrews says, "the word of God is sharper than any two-edged sword, piercing between bone and marrow or between the thoughts and intentions of the heart." (v 4:12). If we ask God, He will show us.

So… Arise and awaken! Come out of your stupor. Come to your senses and ask God, "Show me the ultimate intention of my heart!"

Let's go for it! Let's dive in, yes, *All In!*

"Whether you eat or drink or whatever you do, do all to the glory of God" (1 Cor. 10:27). All that we do—how we respond to conflict, how we treat others, if we forgive, pay bills, live responsibly, or whatever we do—is an essential expression and is building a kingdom. If we submit ourselves to Jesus, the ultimate intention of our hearts' will build the Kingdom of God.

In the original tabernacle, the High Priest was charged with a curious task. They had to remove wax deposits from the candles on the golden lampstands. As the wax deposits were removed, the candle's flames would be less obscured and emit more light. Though this job appears pretty mundane for a High Priest, remember much in the Old Testament alluded to greater realities.

In Hebrews, the author tells us that Jesus is the great High Priest (4:14). The temple is no longer a building, but within us believers (2 Cor. 6:16). We are called to shine bright (Matt. 13:43), like brilliant stars (Phil. 2:15), but past sin and wounds from others can leave deposits in our hearts. If we allow Jesus to do His continuing work of sanctification in our hearts, He (*the* High Priest) removes those deposits so we can go all in, shine brighter, and walk in fullness.

Holy Spirit, there is now no more condemnation for those in Christ Jesus! (Rom. 8:1). Lord, reveal to me the ultimate intention of my heart. As the Great High Priest, please reveal the deposits that have built up and remove them so I can shine bright again. The end of all being is not my own happiness. May the ultimate intention of my heart be to love You and build Your kingdom.

Renew my mind, so I'm aware that everything I do can be spiritual worship. That each of my choices support my ultimate intent to love and serve you. Bring me to my senses and grant me the shalom to overcome any distraction from going all in!

———

Download your free *Discussion/Study Guide* for group and individual discipleship. Visit www.kipgaines.com/allin

CHAPTER 5

Biblical Worldview
(God, Angels, and People)

With the proper motivation, let's continue building the foundation of the Biblical Worldview. Again, I think it's really important to break things down to their most basic forms to better understand complicated concepts. If we have an incorrect foundational understanding of who God is and who we were created to be, our perspective (or worldview) will become more and more skewed.

Let's review that framework from Chapter 2.

One Gods—Father, Son, and Holy Spirit

Five Influences—God, the adversary, ourselves, others, and circumstance

Three Heavens—physical realm, the spiritual realm, and the Highest Heaven

Two Kingdoms—the Kingdom of God and the kingdom of the adversary

Three Origins of Thought—us, God, and the adversary

Maybe you think the big questions—like, "Who is God?" or "What's the purpose of my life?"—are too philosophical. What about the question of value?

"Am I valuable?" Our answer to this universal question profoundly affects how we live our lives. Without getting into detail, here's how a couple of prominent worldviews address the question of value.

In the words of a great speaker and friend Winkie Pratney:

In existentialism, there is purpose for the individual and none for the whole. In communism, there's purpose for the whole and none for the individual. But in Christianity, there is purpose for the individual and purpose for the whole. We are saved to serve, and we become part of something far greater than ourselves.

But I'm getting ahead of myself, let's look at the worldview the Bible presents. In order to properly measure our purpose and value, we must establish who God is first.

The Nature and Character of God

According to the Bible, who is God? That is a question that philosophers and theologians have discussed for millennia, but I want to simply focus on two basic aspects: God's being and God's character. God's being is what He's made of, and His character is what He does. What is God made out of? The simple answer is God stuff. I don't mean to be overly simplistic, but remember, I want to focus on the big picture instead of getting bogged down in specifics—especially ones that are impossible to fully understand. Stay with me. Now, what is God stuff?

To answer that, we'll have to start at the beginning, Genesis 1:1, the first five words of the Bible. Most translations read: "In the beginning God created…" Nothing too surprising, but if you look at it in the original Hebrew, something interesting happens. Those first words are: *Beresheeth bara Elohim.*

Let's focus on the word *Elohim* (אלהים). Though our English Bibles translate this as "God," the Hebrew word is more complex, so I'll break it down as we did to the word *shalom*. In Hebrew, *El* (אל) means God or strong authority. The *-im* (ים) ending signals that the noun is masculine plural. The *h* (ה) in the middle denotes a *very*. The word in the original language tells us that God stuff is very strong, plural, and unified—One Gods. These authorities are so unified they are one, but they are also different beings who hold different roles within the Godhead.

The Bible identifies three distinct members of the Godhead: the Father, Son, and Holy Spirit. Now, is Father stuff Son stuff? Or is Son stuff Holy Spirit stuff? No, they are separate beings, but they are all made of God stuff. Is there anything else made out of God stuff? No, because God stuff has unique characteristics. We'll never be able to fully describe it, but the Bible does reveal important traits.

First of all, God is eternal. There are lots of verses that describe God as eternal, forever, everlasting, etc. He is the uncreated Creator and always will be, the beginning and the end, the Alpha and the Omega (Rev. 1:8). As we contemplate eternity, there is both eternity past and eternity future. God alone has always lived in eternity past and He will always live in eternity future as the uncreated. We are so limited, so finite, it's a little difficult to wrap our minds around this, but let me try to illustrate this concept of eternity.

Imagine there's a little bird and this little bird begins to relocate the entire earth. The bird grabs a granule of sand (chirp, chirp) and flies away. It comes back 1000 years later. The bird then grabs a droplet of water or a piece of earth and it flies away. It comes back 1000 years later. Imagine every thousand years this bird keeps transporting another small piece of earth. After a seemingly incomprehensible amount of time, there would come a point in time when the bird was finished relocating the entire earth. The sobering reality is all of eternity future would still be left.

WOW! What a revelation!

So here we have this incredibly unique Godhead where all three have existed in perfect harmony for all eternity past! And all three will continue to exist in perfect harmony for all eternity future.

I think if we could understand just a part of the concept of eternity, we'd realize the seriousness of the choices we make.

Besides eternal, God stuff is omnipresent, right? God can be everywhere at once. ("Where can I go from your Spirit?" Ps. 130:7-12) The Bible also tells us God stuff is omniscient (He knows everything that can be known) (1 John 3:20, Ps. 147:5, Heb. 4:13) and omnipotent (all-powerful) (Jer. 32:27, Matt. 19:26).

Is the Father all-powerful? Yes.

Is the Son? Yes.

Is the Holy Spirit? Yes.

What if they got in a fight, who would win? If they did fight, we'd be in big trouble. But they never will because they can't. How do we know? The root of all conflict is either ignorance or wickedness (or both). We can be confident that God will never get in a fight because He is neither wicked nor ignorant. He can't sin, and He knows everything that can be known, remember?

Now, let's move on to God's character. What does God do with His stuff? There are specific roles that the different members of the Godhead hold, but there is a simple answer. He loves. Love is not a special feeling or something abstract. Love is an attitude of the will. It's a choice to bestow kindness on others according to what is right and proper. It's desiring the highest good for another. God has the intelligence to do the right thing with His stuff. He knows what's best. God does whatever is most loving in any given situation. He is love personified (1 John 4).

At some point, God decided it was most loving to create angels, then people. This brings up something else God can do with His stuff, He creates. He can make stuff out of no stuff. He made angels, and the world around us, out of nothing. If He created all this stuff out of no stuff, why do we worry?

When we were with the natives in the jungles of Belize, we noticed something very interesting about their worldview. In the village we stayed in, clay pots were very important. The villagers would use clay pots to store things, clean in, prepare food, etc. Every so often, the village elders would walk around the village and if they thought someone had too many clay pots, they would break some. Why? The elders thought there was only a certain amount of clay pots. If someone had too many, there wouldn't be enough to go around. Sounds silly, but this is the same basic thought in the communist worldview. There is only so much to go around. If someone has too much we have to break, or take, their "clay pots."

That's **not** how the kingdom of God operates.

God is unlimited in resources and can create stuff out of no stuff. In fact, He spoke the entire universe into existence. Have you met God? If He hasn't radically changed your life, I would say that you haven't. You can't have a causal relationship with someone who speaks the universe into being.

So far, we have a simple overview of who God is. God is made of God stuff, which is triune but one, uncreated, eternal, omnipotent, omnipresent, and omniscient. What God does with His stuff (His character) is love and He can create stuff from no stuff. Everything that God does is the highest good, therefore it's the most loving thing for everyone. Got it? Here's a little chart to help all you visual learners.

IN THE BEGINNING: It all began with One whom had no beginning

Hear oh Israel, the LORD your God is One

Deuteronomy 6:4

Being	**Character**
(the stuff you're made out of)	(what you do with your stuff)
• **Eternal** (no start or finish)	• **Loving**
• **Uncreated** (Creator)	• **Righteous**
• **Omniscient** (really smart)	• **Kind**
• **Omnipotent** (really strong)	• **Merciful**
• **Omnipresent** (all places)	• **Truthful**
• **Spirit** (Supreme)	• **Faithful**
• **Father, Son, Holy Spirit**	• **Wise**
ELOHIM	• **Forgiving**
	• **Unchangeable**

by Kip Gaines

God is the only being that is uncreated. He exists as God stuff. We can't fully describe God stuff, but the Bible clearly declares God as Elohim—Father, Son, and Holy Spirit. They are unique beings, but all three are made of God stuff. They are one (Deut. 6:4) in character (what they do with their stuff) and in ultimate intent.

The Nature and Character of Angels

Now, let's talk about angels. What are angels? We'll break this question down the same way, being and character. What are angels made out of? You guessed it: angel stuff. Angel stuff is different from God stuff. It is created (by God), limited (in power, knowledge, to one location), and seemingly gender neutral. There is nothing stated clearly in the Bible about baby angels—certainly not naked ones flying around with harps. Angels were created in the full presence of God and their beings are neither righteous nor unrighteous. What they do with their stuff (their character) determines if they are righteous or unrighteous.

When God created angels, was there evil in the universe? No, only

God. So, did God create evil? No! Before angels were created evil wasn't a possibility, there was only God and His kingdom. When God created these beings, He created them to be in relationship with Him. To truly be in a loving relationship with God, they needed to have the ability to choose, so logically, the possibility of rebellion came into existence. Only the abstract concept of sin was introduced into the universe as a possibility because God was not the only one making choices. If God did not give angels the ability to choose, they would not be capable of introducing evil, but also, there would be no relationship. God created beings with the ability to choose, but He didn't create the choices they made. Ultimately, God is responsible not for angels' choices, but for the beings themselves. That's why He has to and will punish those who have disobeyed.

This is where the Two Kingdoms began. Before angels were created, there was only one kingdom. After angels were created, there was still only one kingdom, but two influences. However, those two influences were aligned, therefore building the same kingdom. When some angels decided to no longer submit to God and rebel, they began to build another kingdom opposed to God. Now there are two kingdoms we can help establish, God's or the adversary's.

What about Lucifer? Did God create an evil being? No! Ezekiel says that Lucifer was created blameless, but then wickedness was found in him (Ezek. 28:15). His heart became proud (v.17) and he wanted to make himself like God (Isa. 14:14). But what was Lucifer really saying? Was he claiming to be uncreated or that he knew everything or that he was everywhere at once? Of course not, he can't change his being. He couldn't suddenly be made of God stuff.

So, what did he mean?

Lucifer could not accomplish any of his "I will" declarations (Isa.14:13-14) he made, but these reveal his true desire. He basically said, "I want to do what I want to do." He wanted his will to be higher than God's will. When Lucifer said he wanted to be like God, he was really saying, "I think I'm really special and important, more so than God. What I want is supreme. My will, will be done. It's up to me, not God."

Sounds familiar, doesn't it? This is the same rebellion that we humans enter into. When we refuse to submit to God's will we say, "God, what I want is most important. My will is supreme, not yours. I want my will to be done."

We might not say the words, but the choices we make shout, "God, if I want to be a missionary, I will be a missionary. But if I don't, I won't!"

"If I want to be a race car driver, I will be a race car driver."

"I want to have sex because it feels good, so I'm going to have sex. If I fear the consequences enough, then I won't!"

"I will make my own decisions! My own will is supreme! I am supreme."

Even more subtly, Christians are guilty of this when they tell God, "These are my plans God, now bless them!" We should be saying, "God what's your will? How can I bless you?" It's the difference between a child who trusts their Father and one who doesn't. The child who trusts knows their Father is good and everything the Father has is theirs. Those who lack trust believe if they surrender to God, God will cut them short.

So, why should angels submit to God? Is God on a power trip or something? Of course not, God just knows the most loving thing to do in all situations. He created angels to do with their stuff what He does with His stuff. What makes an angel righteous or unrighteous is if they submit to God or not. The angels who do not submit and want their own wills done become demons. Angels who choose to submit to God, to the purpose for which they were designed, choose to do what is most loving: loving God, bringing forth God's purposes, and building His kingdom.

Let's review and look at the God and angel chart side by side.

IN THE BEGINNING: It all began with One whom had no beginning

Hear oh Israel, the LORD your God is One

Deuteronomy 6:4

Being (the stuff you're made out of)	**Character** (what you do with your stuff)
• **Eternal** (no start or finish) • **Uncreated** (Creator) • **Omniscient** (really smart) • **Omnipotent** (really strong) • **Omnipresent** (all places) • **Spirit** (Supreme) • **Father, Son, Holy Spirit** ELOHIM	• **Loving** • **Righteous** • **Kind** • **Merciful** • **Truthful** • **Faithful** • **Wise** • **Forgiving** • **Unchangeable**

by Kip Gaines

ANGEL & DEMON STUFF

Ministering Angels		Demons	
(in all 3 Heavens, part of the Kingdom of God)		(cast into 2nd Heaven, part of the Kingdom of Darkness)	
Being	**Character**	**Being**	**Character**
• Created	• Dependent (submitted)	• Created	• Independent
• Immortal	• Loving	• Immortal	• Unloving
• Limited knowledge	• Righteous	• Limited knowledge	• Accusatory
• Limited power	• Kind	• Limited power	• Divisive
• Limited place	• Merciful	• Limited place	• Selfish
• Not supreme	• Truthful	• Not supreme	• Jealous
	• Wise		• Envious
	• Forgiving		• Bitter
			• Unforgiving

by Kip Gaines

The Nature and Character of People

Ok. Let's move on to people. What are human beings? According to Genesis 2, human beings are made out of dust and God breath. Without getting into scientific specifics, what are people made out of?

If you said "People Stuff" you're catching on. Our physical beings (what we're made of) are created, gender-specific, and limited (in knowledge, power, and to one location). When God created humans in the beginning, He said they were "very good" (Gen. 1:31).

So, if we are very good, why is this world so messed up? Well, we are made of good stuff, people stuff. People stuff is neither righteous nor wicked. Sin isn't a physical issue. No matter how powerful your microscope is, you will never see sin within human cells. What we do with our stuff, our character, determines whether we are righteous or sinful. God created human beings with the ability to think but did not create the thoughts that they think. Likewise, He created humans with the ability to choose but did not create the choices they make.

Like angels, what we choose to do with our stuff makes us righteous or unrighteous. It's not just what we refrain from, that's only part. He is righteous because He loves and everything He does is loving. Also, like angels, God created us to do with our stuff what He does with His stuff. He calls us to love. Remember, love is not an emotional state or a special way of feeling, but an attitude of will. It's a choice to bestow kindness on others according to what is right and proper. Love is desiring the highest good for another.

So how are we actually like God and how are we not like God? If we try to fill His role in our lives, we get in trouble. God is God and we are not. He created us to be in relationship and do with our stuff in miniature what He does with His stuff in magnitude.

We are partakers of the DNA of the Most High God. We do not become Him, but we submit our stuff to Him in such a way that we do with our stuff what He does with His stuff. That's how you become part of the kingdom of God. You cannot be a part of His kingdom in any other way, shape, or form other than through relationship because that's how God designed it. God's way is not just the best way, it is THE way. And He offers us the opportunity to go all in!

God wants us to do in miniature
what He does with His stuff in magnitude.

Another way we resemble God's likeness is we can create. We cannot create something from nothing, but with Him, we can co-create. First, we can co-create other humans. Second, we co-create our thoughts and responses—in other words, our character. Just as with angels, God is not responsible for the development of our character, only to hold us accountable for our choices. This is where blessings and curses come in.

Our character, whether good or bad, is developed by the choices, both big and subordinate, we make each day. When we submit to the Father, we receive an anointing of the Holy Spirit to develop good character. He empowers us to "be holy like He is holy" (Lev. 11:45, 1 Peter.1:16). If we submit our wills to God, day after day, we eventually will be conformed to the image of Jesus. It's God's will that Jesus' words would be true in our lives. "Anyone who has seen me has seen the Father" (John 14:9).

The bottom line is, God wants us to be like Him. He created us in His image, and He wants us to do with our stuff what He does with His stuff. God did not give us an unattainable goal He doesn't hold to. He created us humans to do with our stuff in miniature what He does with His stuff in maximum.

Biblical Worldview (God, Angels, and People)

PEOPLE STUFF

God's Sons & Daughters (transformed by God's love)		Unbelievers (conformed to the world)	
Being	**Character**	**Being**	**Character**
• Created	• Dependent	• Created	• Independent
• Immortal	(submitted)	• Mortal	• Unloving
• Limited	• Loving	• Limited	• Accusatory
knowledge	• Righteous	knowledge	• Divisive
• Limited power	• Kind	• Limited power	• Selfish
• Limited place	• Merciful	• Limited place	• Jealous
• Not supreme	• Truthful	• Not supreme	• Envious
	• Wise		• Bitter
	• Forgiving		• Unforgiving

by Kip Gaines

You may wonder why God chose to do things this way. Even if God didn't create evil, why did He allow the possibility for it? Isn't that basically the same thing? Many use this logic and accuse God of being irresponsible, or maybe just not thinking things through. But let me use a silly illustration to explain. Imagine if I sneak onto my neighbor's farm and steal his scarecrow. Next, I record myself saying, "I love you Kip. I worship you. I want to spend all my days with you." I then hook the audio player to a motion sensor and put it on my little scarecrow buddy. My creation is complete and every time I walk by my scarecrow plays: "I love you, Kip. I love you, Kip." Imagine if I then insist that my buddy really loves me? I'd be crazy, right?

If something is programmed, it cannot give or receive love. Love requires the freedom of choice and therefore demands risk. The only way God could expand love beyond the Godhead required risk. The hope that His creation would choose to love Him is worth the risk of rebellion. Because God loves and wants to be loved, He does not make our choices. God does not choose whether you go to heaven or not, you choose. He has drawn, is drawing, and will continue to draw every single human being to Himself. Every person has the choice to respond. We must have this choice to receive His love and walk in His will or it would not really be love.

I want to end with one illustration, but I need your help. Can you take your nose off? Please? Just take it off and put it down here on the page. Come on, help me out. So, you don't want to do it, huh? Well, if you don't, you can't go to heaven. What's it going to be?

If this silly scenario was real and I had the power to grant eternal life, which one of us would be the idiot or the evil being? Would it be you, the one who can't perform the impossible task? Or me, the one demanding an impossible task? That's right, I would be the stupid, evil being for demanding the impossible. "The commands I put before you are not too difficult nor is it out of your reach" (Deut 30:11). If God asks us to be in relationship with Him and walk out a lifestyle of repentance, it must be possible. He wouldn't ask us to do something we couldn't do. If He did, He would be in the wrong; He would be the stupid or evil one. It is possible for us to do with our stuff in miniature what He does with His stuff in magnitude. He doesn't ask of us anything that He doesn't require of Himself.

As you can see, without this foundational understanding to build upon, it's easy to have a skewed view of the world. When we understand the big picture a little better —have the correct perception of reality, God, etc.—this world makes so much more sense.

So, let's go back to the question of value. What determines our value as individuals? I believe that God made it possible for you to be so valuable, that it transcends your understanding. God came in the form of a man, and He gave His life to allow the potential of relationship. Many don't believe this, so they self-medicate in many forms. They end up destroying their lives presupposing they're not important. Some commit suicide because they don't value themselves or others. If we all made decisions through the lens that we and others are valuable, this world would be a much different place.

Did Christ come and die for you personally? Did He open a door so you can have intimacy with the Creator of the universe? Yes or no? Christ already made a value statement. He made it with His life, death, and resurrection. If you say you are not valuable, you nullify the work of Christ and Him crucified! God made a really loud statement with His life, death, and resurrection: YOU ARE VALUABLE. I don't want to call God a liar, so I need to accept this reality. If you don't feel valuable, the question is not, "Am I valuable?" That question has been answered. The real question is this: "Are you willing to live up to the value that God has provided?"

God calls us valuable and asks us to live up to that value. Whether we choose to assert our supremacy or submit our will determines what kingdom we are building. Those who submit, choose the highest good and help establish God's Kingdom. When we do in miniature with our stuff what He does with His stuff in magnitude, we will both feel fulfilled (for this is why we were created) and have a greater impact on the world around us.

Jesus! Help me to see you for who you truly are and let me see myself the way you see me. Empower me to live a lifestyle of victory. I want to live up to the value that you have provided. I want to submit my will to you because your will is most important. You call me your child. Please indelibly burn this revelation into my heart!

I'm all in. I want to do with my stuff what you do with your stuff. I love you!

———

Download your free *Discussion/Study Guide* for group and individual discipleship. Visit www.kipgaines.com/allin

CHAPTER 6

The Tender Heart of God

Before I begin this chapter, I want to acknowledge my dear friend, Dean Harvey. Giving credit where credit is due is an essential part of humility, as well as being part of the body. Much of this chapter and some illustrations were passed down to me through Dean. He is such an anointed teacher. I still remember his persistent challenge: "I'm glad you know truth! The point is, are you living it?"

Truth is not just concepts, facts, or ideas. Truth is a Person, and His name is Jesus. He is the way, the truth, and the life. Knowing Truth is what set us free. To know truth but not live up to it is not good. If you know truth and resist it, you develop a hardness of heart. Growing cold to truth is about the most dangerous thing that anyone can do. It's the pinnacle of pride, and exactly what Lucifer did.

To the degree that we respond to the conviction of the Holy Spirit in our lives is to the degree we will be conformed into the image of our Lord Jesus Christ. To the degree we resist the conviction of the Holy Spirit in our lives is to the degree we will be conformed into the image of Lucifer. Fully responding and conforming requires a grace only found in covenant. Understanding God's heart behind this covenant He longs to make with us casts a new light on a powerful truth that, for many, has lost meaning.

The scary thing about being raised in church is you hear the truth *a lot*. When you don't respond to truth, you become resistant, or at least numb, to it. Then the power of that truth is lost.

This is one of the reasons why Jesus loved sinners and yelled at the religious people in the Gospels. He expected sinners to sin. When He met sinners in their sin, He showed them true freedom, called them out, and they (mostly) responded. On the other hand, He expected the religious to be holy. The reason that many of the religious leaders didn't respond to Jesus or His call was because they were only playing holy and were numb to truth. They had the form of godliness but denied the power that lies therein (2 Tim. 3:5). They memorized verses and followed tradition to the utmost, but they didn't apply the fullness of truth to their lives. Unfortunately, the same thing happens in our lives, especially when a truth is so often repeated.

Our identity as believers is very clear in the Bible. But this evident truth often becomes distorted or watered down. Being a believer doesn't mean you go to church. It doesn't mean memorizing verses or knowing facts about God. It doesn't mean expressing some artistic gift or a unique position in a church. It means being married, in a covenant relationship with God. We are the Bride of Christ.

Before we can walk in the power of this truth, we must first understand its foundation. When we clearly understand God's heart and desire for relationship, we can fully relate to Him the way He designed. If we are called to be the Bride of Christ, we need a revelation of how our choices affect God's heart

This is Eternal Life

I encourage everyone to memorize John 17:3 because it's a foundational verse in our relationship with God. Jesus said, "Now this is eternal life: that they know You, the only true God, and Jesus Christ, whom You have sent."

So, what is eternal life? Eternal life is fellowship with God. That word *know* in the Greek is the word *ginosko* (γινώσκουσίν), which means experiential knowledge as a present active indicative, or a continuous action in the present. Eternal life is *knowing* God.

If ever there were a word that cried out for a word study, it is *ginosko*. Read John 10:14-16 with this new understanding of experiential, present knowing. Jesus says, "I am the good shepherd. I **know** my own and they **know** me, just as the Father **knows** me and I **know** the Father."

Ginosko functions as the key term describing not only our relationship with the Son and the Father but the Son with the Father (and the Father with the Son). It also shows a correlation between how we know the Father and Son, and how the Son and Father know each other.

Stop for a moment and reflect on that—it's overwhelming. How do you know if you're saved? If you are in relationship with God, if you are *knowing* Him, you are saved. You may know about Him or you may have known Him in the past, but continuously, actively *knowing* God is the key.

We should be continuously experiencing God! Salvation is not a legal transition that takes place in the heavenlies, but the result of holding God's hand through the changes and challenges of life. The Bible is very clear that eternal life is relationship. If you are in relationship, you have eternal life. If you are not in relationship, if you're not knowing God, you don't have eternal life.

Scripturally, you were created for relationship with God. You were designed, knit together uniquely because there's a place in God's heart only you can fill. I have four kids who are all completely different, and I love each of them so much. If one of my daughters, for example, thought I didn't love them and decided not to talk to me, it would be incredibly painful. No one can talk to me like her or love me like her; no one can fill her place. As much as I love my other kids, nobody can relate to me in the place of the other.

I have a little, tiny human heart. God has a massive, eternal heart in which you were created to fill. There's a place in His heart I can't reach, only you can reach. If you're not in relationship with God, I want to suggest that He is the one who suffers most. His desires, His dreams, His vision, and His passion to love and bestow goodness goes unfulfilled. He's the one who hurts the most if you decided not to talk to Him. There's a place in God's heart with your name on it, and if you're not in relationship with God, if you're not relating to Him, then you are bringing brokenness and grief to the heart of God. I'm going to prove this from the word of God later in this chapter.

If you're not in relationship with God,
He is the one who suffers most.

We weren't created for a casual acquaintance but a deep, intimate relationship with our Creator. The analogy that God uses the most in the Bible is a marriage relationship. This gives us the closest tangible picture of what He desires. In the Old Testament, Father God is the Husband and Israel (His people) is the wife. In the New Testament, Jesus is the bridegroom, and the church is the bride. He uses this illustration because it's the closest covenant relationship we have here on earth.

God created us to have our most intimate covenant relationship with Him. He longs for this intimacy with each of us. We don't become the same person, but we live for the same purpose, go in the same direction, and are the greatest testimony to each other's life. In marriage, I should do nothing without involving my wife and having her best in mind. In life, as a lover of God, I should do nothing without involving God and having His highest in mind.

I'm married to the most amazing, incredible woman. We've gone through a lot of hardship, but we have the best marriage in the world. I know and am known by Diana better than anyone else. But guess what? Our intimacy didn't magically happen. At first, we just met. Here's how it happened... I was at a ski lodge, grabbing a drink with my friend, Tom. As we went up to the bar, he noticed Tammy, the girl he liked, across the room. As I followed, sitting in the booth with Tammy sat the most beautiful woman I'd ever seen. My first thoughts were, "I gotta get out of here." I couldn't afford to be distracted or spend money on a girl. Remember, I was set on being a race car driver. That took all I had. I was all in. But fortunately, my friend introduced us. So, I saw Diana, then met her, but did I know her?

We can meet God, but not really know Him yet.

Diana and I spent every evening that week together. Did I know her then? Not really, but I was getting to know her. In the dating stage, people are careful to put their best foot forward, and we wear all sorts of masks. But boy, I was twitterpated. My head was swimming. When you have a crush, everything they do is special—and I had a crush.

After a few dates, we decided to go steady. But even when we were exclusively seeing each other, I was still getting to know her. Then came the day, with a pounding heart, I asked Diana to marry me, and we got engaged. An engagement is the anticipation of a covenant relationship. I was getting to know her more, I really liked her, and I wanted to make that marriage commitment. But it wasn't until the day we were married, that I really started knowing my wife. True intimacy requires commitment.

Our wedding (1979)

You make a covenant when you say, "I do." If you haven't said it, you haven't made the covenant. You can talk about it, you can know all about the ceremony and the process of marriage, but that's not commitment. Likewise, you can know about a person, you can describe them, you can talk about them, but you don't begin knowing who your mate truly is until you are married in a covenant relationship. True intimacy can only break forth through the avenue of covenant. That's the way God designed it. If we try to establish relationship without covenant, it will ultimately lead to bondage. The freedom that comes forth from covenant is the freedom to fully know and be known by your spouse through the changes and challenges of life. You can't get that any other way.

So, where are you in this spectrum with God? Maybe you're dating Jesus. He seems cool and you like Him, but there are others out there. Maybe you'll hang out with Jesus or maybe not if something else is going on. You might really like Jesus and you're giving engagement some serious thought. You've done the whole selfishness thing (or the religious thing) and you are sick of yourself, sick of the Devil, sick of all the junk. You've had it and you're ready to stand up and say, "I do!" **I'm All In!**

Take some time to honestly think about this. Where do you fall in this spectrum? Have you met God? Do you just know about Him? Have you prayed the prayer, think you have a ticket to heaven, and that's all there is? Maybe you've felt something's missing. You've cried out to see God's face with no result, but you've never married Him. God wants to reveal Himself to you, but a deeper level of intimacy requires a deeper commitment.

Let's continue the marriage analogy. Imagine the wedding music playing at a church and the Father and Jesus are up at the altar. Picture the Father as the pastor and Jesus as the groom. I come walking up. The Father starts, "Jesus, do you take Kip, to be your lawfully... from this day forth?"

Jesus says, "I do."

The Father turns to me, "Kip, do you take Jesus..."

"I do."

Father: "Jesus do you have a ring or any sort of symbol to show, to prove your devotion?"

Jesus: "Yes, Father." He shows the scars in His hands and the hole in His side.

"I came to earth, laid aside my attributes of being God, and I laid down my life to prove to Kip that I would never forsake him or betray him or do anything lest I have him in mind."

The Father looks at me. "Kip, do you have a ring or any sort of symbol to show, to prove your devotion?"

Now it's my turn. Oh, shoot. What am I going to do?

I fall to the ground weeping at His feet. How could I do anything less than totally and completely lay down my life and give my everything to Jesus? Anything less, and I would be insulting the love He bestowed upon me.

We get everything and He gets a mess. He gets a recovering sinner. We get to be in a real, close relationship with the One who knows the beginning to the end, loves us perfectly, and allows us to be part of something far greater than we could ever imagine. Now that's exciting.

Have you made that decision? Have you given all of yourself? Have you covenanted yourself to the One who loves you perfectly through the changes and challenges of life? If you haven't, take a moment to really think about this question.

This is serious. Stop reading for a moment to honestly consider and pray.

If you've never truly given all of yourself, but you want to, do it now. Remember, true intimacy breaks forth through covenant. Once we make this covenant, we can truly start knowing God.

If you are completely at a loss about where to start, let me give you a challenge. When I speak, I encourage those who want to commit to Jesus to do something—something bold. Just as I challenge my students, I'll challenge you. If you want to make this covenant to know (*ginosko*) Jesus, then stand up and yell **"I love you, Jesus!"**

Seriously. Do it. Don't let fear of man hold you back. I think God smiles when we love Him more than our dignity.

I'm sure some may think I carried this whole marriage analogy too far. You may agree that we should commit ourselves to God, but you always thought of it more as a legal transaction. You believe God cares but probably not as deeply as I'm describing. Do you believe when you make a decision God is affected? When we sin, does God have a response, or is He so big that it doesn't really matter?

How about when you make a decision to bless or do something righteous, can you sense that heaven is excited? Do your choices have a deep emotional effect on God? If He is personally involved with your life, doesn't that mean He's emotionally involved as well?

God's Emotions Before the Flood

Let's look at Genesis 6:5-6. Though it's not talked about much, I believe that Genesis 6:6 is almost a better representation of God's love for a lost and dying world than John 3:16.

In Genesis 6, creation isn't doing well. "The Lord saw how great man's wickedness on earth had become, and that every intent of his heart was only evil all the time."

In the 1,600 years that elapsed between Gen. 1:1 and Gen. 6:5, theologians estimate there were about 2 billion people on the earth. I guess when you live for hundreds of years you can have a lot of babies. However many people populated the earth at that time, each of them was only motivated by evil. They were just thinking about themselves and their happiness. They didn't pay any attention to God. God walked in the garden with Adam and Eve, and five chapters later, man doesn't want anything to do with Him.

In light of the whole marriage illustration, and knowing that man's choices are affecting God, it's easy to assume God destroyed the earth with a flood because he was angry (and understandably so). But that's not what God was feeling as recorded in the scriptures. Let's look at the next verse.

"The Lord was grieved that he had made man on the earth and His heart was filled with pain" (Gen. 6:6).

Wait a second, God wasn't angry? The Bible says He was grieved. His heart was filled with pain. Choosing to flood the earth wasn't a decision made out of anger, but grief. This truth is profound. God reveals here that He hurts when we sin, and not just a little bit. The Hebrew word for "heart filled with pain," can also mean: to be out of breath and blinded with tears; so upset you're gasping for breath. In Genesis 6, He looked down at the earth and saw His kids, whom He designed for relationship and loved very much. No one but Noah loved Him back or cared about Him at all. Ever love somebody who didn't pay any attention to you?

Sometimes when we think of God and how He's so big and powerful and everywhere at once, we imagine He's too big to be affected by us. If Genesis 6 is true, then we can't begin to comprehend what grief feels like to a Being that feels emotions so massively. God is not too big to feel pain. In fact, He feels more.

Not only that, but grief is in direct proportion to a desire for intimacy. You don't care if you lose something unimportant. Sometimes you don't even realize you've lost it. But how do you feel when you lose something important to you? Especially when that something is someone with whom you desire relationship?

In September of 1983, during the Cold War, a commercial Korean Airliner found itself in restricted USSR airspace. Normal protocol is to contact the plane and send up a couple of fighters to escort it back on track. For whatever reason, a USSR fighter just shot the Korean plane down. At first, the flight was reported missing. Soon it became clear that the unarmed commercial plane was shot down and all 269 Koreans on board were killed.

As I watched the news, leaders from around the world expressed their outrage and denounced this great injustice. They were upset, angry, and vowed to hold the USSR responsible. The scene then switched to a Korean airport, where they announced that Flight 007 had been shot down and there were no survivors. They filmed the reactions of the fathers waiting for their kids, wives waiting for their husbands, and children waiting for their parents. Those who were waiting for their loved ones fell to the ground overwhelmed, blinded by tears, and their hearts were filled with pain.

To the degree that you desire intimacy is to the degree that you experience emotional suffering. Emotional suffering is in direct proportion to the desire for intimacy when that intimacy is lost. Those Koreans were grief-stricken, not angry, because they desired to have intimacy with those who were killed. When God lost the possibility of relationship with those He created and loved in Genesis 6:6, His heart was filled with pain. He was emotionally tied to them, even though they wanted nothing to do with Him.

If we understand the tender heart of God, we'll better understand why Jesus died on the cross. I want to destroy any lies that water down this powerful truth. Genesis 6 shows the heart of the gospel. When God destroyed the earth, He wasn't angry, He was grief-stricken. His heart was filled with pain.

God had hopes and desires and dreams for His children in Genesis 6, but no one wanted anything to do with Him. Throughout the prophetic books in the Old Testament, God expresses how He feels when His people turn away. "How I have been grieved by their adulterous hearts, which have turned from Me, and their eyes, which have lusted after their idols." (Ezek. 6:9) God created us for intimate covenant relationship with Him and we run after other things. How can we begin to understand how that makes Him feel?

Because He loves and wants us to be in relationship with Him, God sent His Son to earth. Jesus, the only something, the only someone, we can point to and say, "That's what God's like." We can look at Jesus, who funneled all that He is into a 5'7" Jewish man. You want to know how God feels about sinners? How did Jesus feel about sinners? What does God feel about religious, pious people? What did Jesus feel about them?

Jesus ministered to people, He touched people at their point of need, He cried, He was engaged emotionally, and He did it all as an exact representation of the Father. He was despised, like His Father. Forsaken, a man of sorrows, a man full of grief, (Isa. 53:3) He reflected the grieved heart of the Father.

What physical suffering is to your body, emotional suffering is to your spirit. The older we get, the more we understand emotional suffering. But no matter how old we are, we understand physical suffering. Therefore, every generation, tongue, and tribe in every place can understand the cross. The crucifixion is applicable because we can all understand physical suffering. If you haven't yet experienced emotional suffering, or you're too hard-hearted, God broke it down to a physical understanding.

The first time I really encountered emotional suffering I was 13. That was a really bad year. My parents struggled through a divorce. Then our house burned down to the ground, and we were left with nothing. I don't know if you've ever experienced a total loss house fire, but the reality is, you don't even have another pair of underwear to put on in the morning. It was no joke. The fire even killed my dog, who was my best friend at the time.

That same year, my grandfather was going through a lot of hard stuff. My dad and I left for the weekend on some business and my grandfather went into the garage with a 5th of Jack Daniels, stuffed the registers, and let the car run. We found him three days later.

I remember, as a 13-year-old who only understood physical suffering up to that point, weeping in the back of our car crying, "Why? Why did grandpa do that? I don't understand." I felt that same "out of breath, blinded by tears" feeling. It was the first time I understood emotional suffering.

> *What physical suffering is to your body,*
> *emotional suffering is to your spirit.*

Several years later, I was working at my dad's shop. He had a machinist shop where I made electrodes. Electrodes are 6-foot long by 8-inch diameter rods of graphite (think huge pencil lead) that we put in a big machine to turn them down to 8 inches +/- .010 of an inch. One day I was working a couple of machines at once. I was at the lathe, polishing an electrode, and BAM! I cut off the end of my finger.

The piece of bone at the end of my finger was hanging on by a string and blood was squirting out with my heartbeat. I walked into the next room for help. My coworker John, the only other guy there, fell down to his knees and almost passed out when he saw all the blood. Luckily, he pulled himself together and drove me to the hospital.

When I got to the hospital, I was bleeding everywhere. An Asian doctor, who couldn't speak English very well, said a bunch of stuff I couldn't understand and wrapped a rubber band around the end of my finger. Still talking, he took the piece of my finger, put it in my hand, and wrapped the whole thing up. I thought I was coming to the hospital for help! All I got was a rubber band, a wrapped hand with a piece of finger inside, and a doctor whose only word I could understand was amputation. I was terrified.

Thankfully, a nurse walked up and explained, "The doctor said we don't deal with amputations here, so we are transferring you to a plastic surgeon." They put me in an ambulance and took me to Dr. Taddio, the same plastic surgeon who repaired my face after an earlier stock car wreck. Boy, was I glad to see him.

But when Dr. Taddio looked at my finger, he gave me some bad news. Though he was almost certain my finger wouldn't retake, because I had severed the main artery, the law required him to reattach it. That meant he had to sew on now; but eventually, it would start to rot, and he'd have to cut it off again. I tried to convince him to just throw it out the window, or in the trash, or something, but that didn't work.

There was some good news. I had just started dating Diana, so when I got back home, she took care of me. We spent lots of time together. That was the only bright spot.

I'm not sure if you've ever experienced an injury like this, but as soon as the anesthesia wore off, all I could feel was a throbbing pain in my finger. I felt every heartbeat in my little finger. Boom-boom. Boom-boom. Boom-boom. I even tried tying my hand to the bedpost at night to keep it elevated enough to get some sleep. It didn't work. For two weeks my finger throbbed, and then it got darker and darker.

One morning I woke up and… no throb. What a relief! It was amazing not to feel that throb in my finger anymore. I had a follow-up appointment later that day, but nothing could ruin such a great day, right? Dr. Taddio took one look and knew the finger end didn't take. I had a quick, outpatient surgery to remove it. As I came to in the recovery room, the first thing I noticed was: Boom-boom. NOOOOOO!!

What physical suffering is to your body, emotional suffering is to your spirit. If someone came up to me and said, "Son, I'm going to give you two choices. Either we cut off the end of your other pinky or you can experience the emotional suffering that you experienced when your grandpa committed suicide." Without hesitating, I'd yell, "Here! Take the finger! Take the finger!" Emotional wounds are much more painful than physical wounds and usually take longer to heal.

Jesus went to the cross and made a one-time physical demonstration of the grief the Godhead feels over the rejection from His children. What the cross was to Jesus' physical body was a representation to try to wake us up. Though it's insufficient, the cross reveals the emotional suffering God experiences over the rebellion of man. Because His desire for intimacy is the greatest, God's vulnerability and degree of suffering is also the greatest.

What Grieves Your Heart Most?

Several years ago, I led an incredible missions trip to Puerto Rico. We had the great privilege of seeing real revival break out. People flooded the alters to repent. God moved in power and it was awesome! During that same time, my wife had some incredible personal revelations at home. When I got back, we decided to get a hotel room and share with each other all that God had done. We were so fired up we grabbed a pad of paper and started praying passionate prayers. "Jesus, we love You so much, we'll do anything. Whatever it is God. Whatever is on Your heart, that's what we want to do. Is it discipleship issues? Politics? The abortion issue? God, what do You want us to do? What grieves Your heart the most?"

The answer to the last question was so clear. We both sensed Him say, "It's when I'm left out." That wasn't really what we were asking, but we wrote it down and continued to cry out for direction.

"God we'll do anything!" We were so excited about all that God did in the last weeks we were ready to do anything.

He spoke again. "The thing that grieves me most isn't those issues. It's when I'm left out. If I get involved, I can turn the government around. If I get involved, people quit having abortions. If I get involved, discipleship will happen. All you have to worry about is, never leave me out."

The only thing that God asks of you
is that you don't leave Him out.

This reality is so simple, yet so powerful. The most harmful thing you or I can do to the heart of God isn't making a particular choice. It's simply leaving God out. No matter where you are or what you're doing, if you include Him, He can accomplish things in and through you that aren't dependent on circumstances.

Being conscious to include God isn't always easy at first. Prior to salvation, we are so occupied with ourselves, and our will is most important. Even after salvation, it's harder to live for Jesus than die for Him. Living for Him is really dying to self, day by day. We need to actively know Him presently, continuously. But including God is a process. Including God, or knowing God, isn't living a perfect life. It's living in relationship with Jesus and allowing Him to expose who we are in light of who He is. If we commit our hearts, our will, to Him, we'll be conformed to His image. Then His will becomes ours. The only thing that God asks of you is that you don't leave Him out.

We all have times of crisis in our lives where we just need the comfort that God understands, and that other people don't take lightly what we're going through. These times are the greatest opportunities for us to have incredible intimacy. Jesus experienced this intense intimacy when he was on the cross. To take the cross lightly is quite offensive to the one who endured the agony for our sake.

There was a physician who wrote an article about the passion of Christ from a medical point of view. I wanted to share it with my students, but the author used lots of complicated medical jargon. So I wouldn't lose people, my secretary, Gretchen, and I rewrote it into simpler terms. Although we left out very large medical words, we maintained the integrity of the context.

We must not take the cross lightly.

As we take a deeper look into what was actually happening when Jesus was on the cross, I want us to stop and ask, "God, what did you really go through? How does it make you feel when I take the time to focus on you during your greatest sacrifice? It's not about me right now. It's about You. I don't want to have a distant friendship with you Jesus. You are so worthy of so much more."

Let's go *all in* as we read this article.

"The Crucifixion of Jesus" by Dr. C. Truman Davis

I suddenly realized that I had taken the crucifixion more or less for granted all these years. I had grown callous to its horror through my familiarity with the grim details—and a too distant friendship with him. It finally occurred to me, that as a physician, I didn't even know the actual immediate cause of death. The Gospel writers don't help us very much at this point because crucifixion and scourging were so common during their lifetime. They undoubtedly considered a detailed description totally unnecessary.

I studied the practice of crucifixion itself; that is, the torture and execution of a person by fixation to a cross. Generally, the upright post was permanently fixed in the ground at the site of the execution and the condemned man was forced to carry a heavy crossbar (weighing about 110 pounds) from the prison to the place of execution.

The physical passion of Christ begins in Gethsemane. The gospel of Luke says, "and being in agony he prayed the longer and his sweat became drops of blood trickling down upon the ground." Every attempt imaginable has been used by modern scholars to explain away this phase, apparently under the mistaken impression that this just doesn't happen. A great deal of effort could have been saved by consulting the medical literature. Though very rare, the phenomena of bloody sweat is well documented. Under great emotional stress, tiny capillaries in the sweat glands can break, thus mixing blood with sweat. This process alone produces marked weakness and then shock. Medical attention is necessary to prevent hypothermia.

After his arrest in the middle of the night, Jesus is brought before the Sanhedrin and Caiaphas the high priest. It is here that the first physical trauma is inflicted. A soldier strikes Jesus across the face for remaining silent when questioned by Caiaphas. Then the palace guards blindfold him and mock him. They taunt him saying, "Identify us," as they pass by, spitting on him and striking him in the face.

In the early morning, Jesus, battered and bruised, dehydrated, and exhausted from a sleepless night, is taken to Jerusalem to be scourged and crucified. It was very unusual for a scourging to come before crucifixion. Many scholars believe that Pilate originally ordered flogging as Jesus' full punishment, and later gave in to the angry mob.

Preparations for scourging were carried out as follows: the prisoner was stripped of his clothing and his hands were tied to a post above his head. It is doubtful whether the Romans made any attempt to follow the Jewish law in the matter of scourging. The Jews had an ancient law prohibiting more than 40 lashes. The Pharisees, always making sure that the law was strictly kept, insisted that only 39 lashes be given (in case of a miscount). Historically, scourging was so traumatic, convicts often died a few days after their beating due to blood loss, infection, etc.

The Roman soldier steps forward with a whip consisting of several heavy, leather thongs with two small balls of lead attached near the end of each. The whip is brought down with full force, again and again, across Jesus' shoulders, back, and legs. At first, the heavy thongs cut through the skin only. Then, as the blows continue, they cut deeper into the tissue underneath. This causes blood to ooze from capillaries and veins of the skin, and finally spurting arterial bleeding from the vessels in the underlying muscle. The small balls of lead first produce large, deep bruises which are broken open by subsequent blows. Finally, the skin on Jesus' back is hanging in long ribbons, and the entire area is an unrecognizable mass of torn, bleeding tissue. When the centurion in charge determines that the prisoner is near death, the beating is finally stopped. The half-fainting Jesus is then untied and allowed to slump to the stone pavement, sopping wet with his own blood.

The Roman soldiers see a great joke in this unsophisticated, narrow-minded Jew claiming to be a king. They throw a robe across his shoulders and place a stick in his hand for a scepter. They still need a crown to make their ridiculous representation complete. A small bundle of flexible branches covered with long thorns (commonly used to start fires) is wrapped into the shape of a crown and then pressed into Jesus' scalp. Again, there is massive bleeding, the scalp being one of the most vascular areas of the body.

After mocking him and striking him across the face, the soldiers take the stick from his hand and strike him across the head, driving the thorns deeper into his scalp. Finally, they tire of their sadistic sport and rip the robe from Jesus' lacerated back. This would have already become stuck to the clots of blood and serum in his wounds. Its removal, just as the careless removal of a surgical bandage, causes excruciating pain, and almost as though he was being whipped again Jesus' wounds reopen and bleed.

The heavy crossbar of the cross is then tied across Jesus' shoulders. The procession of the condemned Christ, the two thieves, and the execution detail of the Roman soldiers begins its slow journey along the road to Golgotha. In spite of Jesus' effort to walk erect, the weight of the heavy wooden beam, together with the shock produced by copious blood loss, is all too much. Jesus stumbles and falls to the ground. The rough wood of the beam gouges into the lacerated skin and the muscles of his shoulders. Jesus tries to rise, but his human muscles have been pushed beyond their endurance. The centurion, anxious to get on with the crucifixion, selects a strong, well-built North African onlooker, Simon of Cyrene, to carry the cross. Jesus follows, still bleeding and sweating the cold and clamming sweat of shock until the 650-yard journey is completed. Jesus is stripped of his clothing, except for a loincloth which is allowed for the Jews.

The crucifixion begins. Jesus is offered wine mixed with myrrh, a mild pain-killing mixture, but he refuses to drink. Simon is then ordered to place the crossbar on the ground and Jesus is thrown backward, with his shoulders against the wood. The soldier feels for the depression at the front of Jesus' wrist. He drives a heavy, square, wrought-iron nail through the wrist and deep into the wood. Quickly, he moves to the other side and repeats the action. The soldier is careful not to pull the arms too tightly, but to allow for some flexion and movement. The crossbar is then lifted in place at the top of the upright post and the board reading "Jesus of Nazareth, King of the Jews" is nailed in place.

Jesus' left foot is pressed backward against his right foot. With both feet extended, toes down, a nail is driven through the arch of each, leaving his knees moderately flexed. Jesus is now crucified. As he slowly sags down with more weight on the nails in the wrist, excruciatingly fiery pain shoots along his fingers and up his arms to explode in his brain—the nails in the wrists put pressure on the median nerves. As he pushes himself upward to avoid the stretching torment, he places his full weight on the nail going through his feet. Again, this causes searing agony as the nail tears through the nerves between the metatarsal bones of His feet.

At this point, another phenomenon occurs. As the arms fatigue, great waves of cramps sweep over the muscles, knotting them up in deep, relentless, throbbing pain. With these cramps comes a growing inability to push himself upward. Hanging by his arms, the pectoral muscles are paralyzed, and the intercostal muscles are unable to act. Air is drawn into His lungs, but he cannot exhale. Jesus fights to raise himself in order to get even one, short breath. Carbon dioxide builds up in his lungs, then his bloodstream and his cramps would partially subside. Spasmodically, he is able to push himself upward to exhale and breathe in the life-giving oxygen.

It was undoubtedly during these periods that he uttered the sentences which were recorded: Jesus looking down at the Roman soldiers throwing dice for his seamless garment, said "Father forgive them for they know not what they do." In Luke 23:34, it is a continuous present indicative verb, which means that he kept saying it. He repeated himself.

To the thief hanging on the cross next to him, "Today you will be with me in paradise."

Looking down at the terrified, grief-stricken adolescent John: "Behold your mother." Then, turning to Mary his mother, "Behold your son."

The next cry was a Jewish reference to Psalm 22. "My God why have you forsaken me?" The Jewish leaders recognize that Psalm as a prophecy about the Messiah.

Jesus experiences hours of limitless pain, cycles of twisting, joint-rending cramps, intermittent partial affixation, searing pain as tissue is torn from his lacerated back as he moves up and down against the rough timber. Then another agony begins. As deep, crushing pain deep in his chest as his pericardium slowly fills with serum and begins to compress his heart.

It is now almost over. The loss of tissue fluid has reached a critical level. Jesus' compressed heart is struggling to pump heavy, thick, sluggish blood into his tissue. His tortured lungs are making a frantic effort to gasp in small gulps of air. Then the markedly dehydrated tissues alert His brain. Jesus gasps, "I thirst." A sponge soaked in cheap wine, which is the staple drink of the Roman soldiers, is lifted to his lips. He apparently doesn't take any of the liquid.

The body of Jesus is now extended to the extreme. He can feel the chill of death creeping through his tissues. This realization brings out his next words, probably not much more than a tortured whisper: "It is finished." His mission of atonement has been completed. Finally, he can allow his body to die.

With one last surge of strength, he once again presses his torn feet against the nail, straightens His legs, takes a deeper breath, and utters his final cry: "Father, into Thy hands I commit my spirit."

A healthy man could survive for days on a cross, but in order that the Sabbath not be profaned, the Jews asked for the condemned men to be removed. The common method of ending a crucifixion was breaking the bones in the legs. This prevented the victim from pushing himself upward. The tension could not be relieved from the muscles of his chest and rapid suffocation would occur. They broke the legs of the first thief, and he quickly suffocated. They broke the legs of the second thief, and he also suffocated. But, when they came to our Lord Jesus Christ, they saw this was unnecessary. He had already died.

Apparently, to make doubly sure, the soldier drove his lance through the fifth interspace between the ribs, upward through the pericardium, and into Jesus's heart. The 34th verse of the 19th chapter of the gospel according to Saint John: "And immediately there came out blood and water." There was an escape of watery fluid from the sack surrounding Jesus' heart, and blood from the interior of His heart. Therefore, we have rather conclusive post-mortem evidence that our Lord Jesus Christ died not of the usual crucifixion death by suffocation, but of heart failure due to the shock and constriction of the heart by fluid in the pericardium.

This all happened during the Passover celebration. All around Jerusalem, the Jewish people are slaughtering their lamb for the Passover dinner while God's lamb was crucified as a means for all men to be reconciled to God.

The physical suffering of Jesus is not the atonement. He is our representation of God's grief over our sin. We all understand physical suffering. What physical suffering is to the body, emotional suffering is to the spirit. Jesus was our physical representation, revealing the grief God feels when we live in rebellion. When we live for ourselves, we destroy the hopes, the dreams, and the future plans God has for us. Sin is so destructive!

Did you read Jesus' cause of death? He did not die from the results of crucifixion He did not die of suffocation. Jesus died of anguish of soul, feeling the betrayal, stupidity, rejection, and blindness of the pride of man rejecting Him! He did not die of a lack of strength. He did not die of a lack of willpower. Jesus died of a broken heart. The cross was a one-time, visual demonstration for every nation, every tribe, every tongue to understand the grief that sin causes.

What you just read demands a response. Jesus gave His all. How can we take that for granted? Worthy is the Lamb that was slain to receive the just reward of your suffering (Rev. 5:12).

I'm sorry, Lord. I don't want to be callous to truth. I don't want to take your sacrifice on the cross for granted. I don't want to bring more grief to your heart. Thank you for this revelation of your heart, continue to make it more real.

Thank you, Jesus. Thank you for everything. I'm sick of a distant friendship. Jesus, I want to know you, to live my life knowing you, and lay down my all for you. I want to bring joy to your heart. I LOVE YOU JESUS!!

CHAPTER 7

The Most Valuable Gift

When we go all in with God—when we receive Jesus' sacrifice for our sin and allow Him to be Lord of our lives—He calls us to something far greater, deeper, bigger than we can ever imagine. The personal cost will be far greater than we anticipate because we must die to ourselves continually. On the other hand, the benefits will be far richer and more fulfilling. One unbelievable benefit of our submission is the indwelling Holy Spirit. Let's take a closer look at the Holy Spirit's role and ministry in our lives.

In John 14, Jesus promises the Spirit of Truth to all who love Him and keep His commands. He calls this Holy Spirit a comforter (or advocate) to help, a teacher of all things, and a reminder of Jesus' words and actions. In other gospels, Jesus makes a similar statement about the Holy Spirit who brings divine inspiration when faced with opposition (Mark 13:11 & Luke 12:12). Later, Jesus speaks of peace when He imparts the Holy Spirit to the disciples in John 20:20, a peace that passes understanding and provides the security of salvation.

The Greek word John uses here is *parakletos*, which means helper, comforter, advocate. The Holy Spirit helps us to understand and recall Jesus' words and He comforts by aligning our lives with God's *shalom*. He does not only come upon us for a specific task or position, like in the Old Testament but dwells inside all those who are doing with their stuff what God does with His stuff. This indwelling is the reason Jesus said even "the least in the kingdom of heaven" is greater than John the Baptist (Matt. 11:11). This Spirit gives our spirit new life, we are born again, by which we call out "Abba, Father." He gives us salvation and the confidence that we are adopted into God's family, making us co-heirs with Christ (Rom. 8).

As saints (believers), what is our inheritance? In Ephesians 1:18, Paul prays for us believers, that our eyes "may be enlightened in order that you may know the hope to which he has called you, the riches of his glorious inheritance in his holy people, and his incomparably great power for us who believe." Let's look at this closer. This hope, to which we are called, is the same hope that God shares through Jeremiah: plans for a hope and a future (29:11). We are no longer slaves or orphans, but children of the Most High called to resemble our Father. We are called to be holy as He is holy (1Peter 1:15). That's definitely a bigger job than we can handle alone, which is why the Father sent a Helper. He not only helps us be who God created us to be, but also imparts gifts (inheritance) and "incomparably great power."

In the church today, there are two prominent points of confusion here. The first concerns this incomparably great power, which we will discuss in more detail next chapter. Many denominations believe that once you are saved and you receive the Holy Spirit, you receive His fullness, and therefore there is nothing else to receive. As we'll talk about later, John the Baptist and Jesus clearly spoke of two different baptisms. John's baptism was different than the baptism of the Holy Spirit. The impartation of the Holy Spirit in John 20:20 for the peace of salvation was different from the impartation given in Acts 2. Also, Acts 19 tells us about believers who were baptized for salvation but didn't receive the empowerment of the Holy Spirit until Paul showed up. There's much more to discuss here, but I'll save that for the next chapter.

The second point surrounds our inheritance with the fruit and gifts of the Spirit. There is much confusion over what is the Holy Spirit's role and what is our responsibility. When our worldview is skewed in this area, it causes agitation to our soul. God is God and I am not. If we try to fill the Holy Spirit's role, we become frustrated because it's impossible for us to fill. On the other hand, if we expect the Holy Spirit to fulfill our responsibility, we become frustrated and wonder why things aren't happening. We must examine God's word to understand our responsibilities and which are the Holy Spirit's.

Remember, to keep it simple. Our being is what we are made of (people stuff) which God created with the ability to choose. Our character is what we do with our stuff, the choices we make. We were created to do with our stuff in miniature what God does with His stuff in magnitude. As believers, we can pray that the Holy Spirit helps us make right choices, but ultimately, the development of our character is up to us. The Holy Spirit will influence, but not violate our free will. He brings things to our remembrance, even shows us a way out of temptation (1 Cor. 10:13), but it's up to us to choose. The development of our character is our responsibility.

Now, the development of our character doesn't only mean making right choices. Many believe they only need to make right choices to get into heaven. However, without the Spirit, my right choices will only bear the fruit of Kip. It's about the ultimate intent of the heart. Jesus made it clear that the Pharisees, those who followed the law to the extreme through making right choices, were not a part of His Kingdom. The Pharisees wanted to get into heaven on their own terms. They didn't want to fully submit and be in relationship with God.

God is the only one who knows the highest universal good in all situations. If we submit and commit to a relationship with Him, we gain His perspective—the highest universal good. Outside of relationship with God, only human love is possible. Human love is limited in perception, often selfish, and leads to having sympathy for evil out of human compassion.

Now, if the Spirit of God is not present in your life, you need a law to delineate right and wrong. That's why God gave His people instruction (the Torah) in the Old Testament. If you don't have the indwelling Spirit, certain things (i.e. don't worship other gods, kill people, or commit adultery) need to be clarified. External government is necessary to provide a standard.

When you partake of this heavenly gift of constant communion with God, your conscience is renewed, and you don't need a law. Why not? Because you love. The reason I don't cheat on my wife is because I love her, not because of some Bible verse. If you need the law to tell you not to cheat on your wife, you don't love your wife. You may want her for whatever reason, but you don't really love her; you aren't willing her highest universal good. Because I love my wife, I want to honor her and our relationship. That is the reason I don't cheat on her or even fantasize about other women. I don't need another reason. If you love your brother, you won't take his stuff. If you love God, you aren't going to cheat on Him and worship something else. These wrong choices are not even an option if you truly love.

The Fruit

Just as God loves and manifests the rest of the fruit (joy, peace, patience, kindness, goodness, faithfulness, gentleness, and self-control) in all He does, we are called to do the same. As believers, we manifest the fruit of the Holy Spirit. It's a natural outcome of the indwelling Spirit; however, it's not always that simple. The problem is we came from a place of darkness into light. Before we committed our lives to Jesus, we acted and reacted in certain ways that are still ingrained in our brains. Now, this isn't an excuse to keep sinning. It's a reality to be aware of so we can take the necessary steps to change. That which is natural can become unnatural and that which was unnatural can become natural.

If the fruit of the Spirit isn't manifest in our lives, if our lives aren't fruitful, there are practical steps we must take. For a season of my life, I took Galatians 5 and prayed something like: "God, it says here that love is the fruit of the spirit. In the name of Jesus, I pray for the spirit of revelation, wisdom, and knowledge to know what it means to love. And I ask that love would be the primary motivation for all I do. God, baptize me in the Holy Spirit and well up a spirit of love. And please, tell me what to do that's loving."

As I waited, sometimes God would say something like, "Buy your wife flowers." Whatever He spoke, I did. The next day, I would pray something very similar. "God, give me a greater understanding of what it means to love... Give me a practical application of how I can manifest love." As I asked and obeyed, soon that which was unnatural became natural. Now, almost every morning, my first thoughts are to encourage my wife. It has become so natural I don't have to try to love; it just happens. I'm not following some rule. I'm being sensitive to the Holy Spirit.

*That which is natural can become unnatural
and that which is unnatural can become natural*

When love became more ingrained in me, I moved on to joy. I prayed a similar prayer to allow the Holy Spirit to teach me how to walk in joy. "God give me a greater understanding of joy, a practical application for my life, and teach me to bring joy to those around me." This, along with the rest of the fruit, eventually became a natural part of my life as I consistently asked the Holy Spirit and obeyed. Every believer is somewhere in this process.

That which is natural can become unnatural and that which is unnatural can become natural. Even if it's natural for you to be a selfish, self-absorbed individual who wants to suck the life out of others because of your own bitterness and hurt, you can pray prayers like I did. God will work through the ministry of the Holy Spirit and as you obey, you will walk in the fruit of the Spirit. Your heart, your thoughts, your very spirit will change. If we allow the Holy Spirit to do His cultivating work and we're sensitive to His leading, His fruit will be the natural manifestation. Let us strive to be perfect as our Father, continually growing in character and being faithful with what He's entrusted to us. The Holy Spirit is our Helper, but the bearing fruit of the Spirit (our character) is our responsibility to bear.

Another way to build your character is to spend time with people of character. We become like those around us. This reminds me of my dear friend, Wick. Wick is a YWAM leader, an excellent teacher, and, just like the rest of us, has his own quirks. While teaching, he had this habit of using a unique hand motion as if pulling the words from his forehead, saying "Go figure!" Once, while I was teaching, I caught myself doing the same exact thing. I didn't mean to. I wasn't trying to steal his body language or anything, it just happened. This sort of thing happens to all of us. You reflect or become like who you admire. I'm not talking about being someone's puppet, but like how friends pick up each other's mannerisms.

The most important being to spend time with is the One with perfect character. When you hang out with Jesus, you become like Jesus. It's also important to intentionally spend time around men and women who challenge and encourage you. If you want to have an incredible, intimate relationship with Jesus, it helps to be around others with that kind of relationship. The more time you place yourself in an inspiring environment, the more your character will grow.

Though the gifts of the Spirit are more God's responsibility, the same concept holds true. This phenomenon goes beyond similar sayings and character. It extends to spiritual attributes as well. This reminds me of a YWAM team that partnered with Lou Engle and the Justice House of Prayer in Washington DC. Lou rocks when he prays, and I noticed that some of our team began doing the same; more importantly, they became fervent intercessors. If you want to learn how to intercede, spend time with intercessors. If you desire to be an evangelist, hang out with people who evangelize effectively. If you want the gift of healing or prophecy..., you get the picture. When you hang out with Jesus, you become like Jesus.

The Purpose of Gifts

Before we get into the different spiritual gifts, it's important to understand their purpose. Let's start with the parable of the talents (Matt. 25:13-20). In this parable, a wealthy man (God) goes on a trip and entrusts his servants with different sums of money (talents). To the first he gives five talents, to the second he gives two, and the third servant receives one. In our culture of equality, this may offend some people. Why would one servant get five and another only one? This highlights a very important truth about the kingdom. Though we are all loved equally, not every person is created with the same capacity. "We have different gifts according to the grace given each of us" (Rom. 12:6, Eph. 4:7). This is the wisdom of God; a body of all hands cannot function. We all have different roles to fill and God, in His mercy, only asks us to fulfill the roles He created for us. The most useful gift is the one that is needed at the time.

As a leader of training schools for many years, I saw this reality with my staff. Some were great multitaskers while others were not. Sometimes I had both extremes. During staff meetings I would assign several tasks to one staff member and only one task to another. That was the most loving for both, as the first quickly got bored with a single task and the second got easily overwhelmed. Each task was important and needed to be accomplished well for our school to run smoothly. Similarly, each part of a healthy body performs different functions at different capacities, but all are important.

The most useful gift is the one
that is needed at the time.

This is the primary purpose of the gifts of the spirit: to prepare God's people for service, so the Body of Christ (the Church) may be whole and mature. The gifts are not for our own personal edification. Now, we are all individuals before God with a unique call on our life. However, when we function as individuals, apart from the body, we are susceptible to accusation and deception. This causes us to feel less valuable than we are or become prideful, having too high an estimation of ourselves.

This is what happened to Lucifer. Details aside, he felt like his gifting was more valuable than others', and his will was more important than God's will. He thought he was more important than other angels and then decided he was more important than God. This is the same spirit of pride that causes you or I to believe our gifting is more important than another's.

Unfortunately, this mindset is too often found in today's church. That's really sad. When we realize that we all have different anointings, different parts to play, then we can join together as the Body of Christ and function at full capacity. This is what the gifts of the Spirit are all about.

There is no power play in the Godhead. The Father doesn't reign back the Others, reminding them He has authority over the times and the seasons (Acts 1:7). Though Jesus submits to the Father, the Father doesn't dominate over Jesus. They all recognize the roles they each hold and are interdependent on one another. That is why it's important to realize our particular ministries and fulfill them in humility.

There's another important point is in the parable of the talents (Matt. 25). The servants who were faithful with what they were given were entrusted with more. If we are faithful to exercise the gifts God entrusts to us, no matter how small we think they are, He can entrust us with more. It is possible to grow our capacities. On the other hand, the servant who was not faithful with his one talent had it taken away, and he was kicked out. Even if we don't think our part is as important as others, we are still called to be faithful.

Desiring gifts and being willing to receive is important, but we must faithfully build our character. I can pray, "Oh God, give me the gift of healing." Seeking more is good, and that's a gift only God can give. God will usually answer, "Oh Kip, establish your character first, so I can entrust you with more." That makes sense, right? It is more dangerous to be surrounded by people with lots of gifts and bad character, than those with character and limited gifts. Who would you rather be around?

When we just focus on gifting, it's dangerous. Our eyes get fixed on the temporal and taken off the eternal. Paul encourages believers to "follow the way of love and eagerly desire spiritual gifts" (1 Cor. 14:1). These steps need to be kept in order, so our focus is on the Giver, not the gifts. It's not wrong to desire gifts but following faithfully is more important.

Thankfully, perfect character isn't necessary to be entrusted with gifts. God uses imperfect people, both in the scriptures and today. As we'll see in the covenant chapter, God's looking for those who are willing. We must intentionally build our character, willingly receive what He gives us, and be faithful with what we have. Then we can know Him in greater ways and be entrusted with more.

The Five-Fold and more

Now let's focus on the gifts. There are several scriptures where spiritual gifts are mentioned; one set is referred to as the five-fold ministry (Eph. 4). Paul says that the Holy Spirit anoints some to be apostles, some to be prophets, some to be evangelists, some pastors, and some teachers. The people holding these offices are God's gift to the world. Why? These gifts are given by God to prepare His people for service so that the body of Christ may be built up, unified, and mature (v12-13). The reason God gives you pastoral gifting is not just so you can be a pastor and be fulfilled in your pastorate. It's not only so you can have a function or a place where you fit in the Body of Christ. Yes, this does happen, but you're called to build up the Body. If you believe that your position is meant to bring you personal fulfillment, you are headed for a wreck. There will be plenty of times that your position will not feel fulfilling. But when you under-stand your role is given for the building up of the Body, then you better understand your function. There's a big difference between the humanist perspective (life's purpose is the happiness of man) and seeing you're a part of something way bigger than yourself.

So, with these ministries, where do electricians fit? We need electricians. Many people, the Church included, like to separate the sacred and secular though this is inconsistent with scripture. We need electricians that love Jesus. Remember the Ultimate Intent chapter? Everything we do should be motivated by our love for God. With the right heart motivation, an electrician can bring just as much joy to the heart of God as a missionary.

God has gifted us with practical abilities, but we all need to build the Body as well. As we serve the body physically, let us use the gifts God gives to serve spiritually too. As Christians, we are called to be ministers of the gospel primarily and also be faithful with our God-given talents.

God gave an incredible revelation to my dear friend Winkie Pratney. A few years ago, Winkie had a bad fall right before traveling to South Korea. On the airplane, he began to experience incredible pain and got very, very sick. When the plane landed, he was taken immediately to the hospital where they found that he had perforated his intestines. Toxins had leaked into his abdominal cavity, and he needed emergency surgery. Repairing his intestines required intensive surgery and there was a period of time when he clinically died. The doctors revived him and after recovering, he recounted his incredible experience.

This is what he shared at a YWAM staff conference:

I've heard that when some people have a near-death experience, they see light at the end of a tunnel. Everything was white. There was no tunnel, no light at the end of a tunnel. I wondered, maybe Jesus would appear on my right side with His arm around me, revealing the mysteries of eternity. But Jesus was not to my right. Then I thought, maybe the Father would come on my left, put His arm around me, showing him what was to come. But the Father didn't come. Well, surely I'll hear the voice of the Holy Spirit is behind me saying, "Well done, Winkie. This is the way, go therein." But there was no voice.

In a moment, like a blink, I realized He was inside of me. I was looking through His eyes and saw the world through the eyes of God! Then I was alive again.

Wow! That's "Christ within, the hope of glory." (Col. 1:27) Christ was in him, and He saw the world through the eyes of God.

Winkie then said:

> I'm so glad we are not all the same. What would the world be like with no stone cutters? There would be no Sistine Chapel. What if we were all stone cutters? There would be no one to paint the interior of the chapel. What if we were all accountants? What if there were no accounts? What a crazy world this would be. What if we were all policemen? What if there were no policeman?

When God raised up Israel to be the very first non-pagan nation, He called both the secular and sacred together. The prophet, the priest, the king, the artist, the stone cutters, the mathematicians, etc. were all called to be His people. When Winkie saw the world through the eyes of God, he saw the incredible intrinsic value of each and every individual reflecting different aspects of God.

WOW! God, may we realize the incredible roles and responsibilities we each have making up your body.

Do you realize the magnitude of what you are part of? You are part of something so far greater than yourself. You're part of the remnant of God, from every nation, every creed, color, and background. Rich and poor, first world to third world, Jew and Gentile, young and old, married and single, educated and simple, strong and weak, trained and untrained, from stone cutters to dancers, from musicians to mechanics, from newborn to patriarchs, WE ARE ALL CALLED according to His purpose. No child of God is excluded; we will all come together, offering our unique expression as we reflect the glory and character of God. With one spirit, one voice, one heart, we'll worship God and raise up His banner before All Nations! This is what we become part of when we go *all in*. AMEN!

Motivational Gifts

Another set of gifts, found in Romans 12, is called motivational gifts. The gifts of prophecy, serving, teaching, encouragement, giving, leading, and mercy are given according to the grace God gives us. Here, Paul talks about the importance of each member of the Body playing their role for the glory of God. Each of these gifts can be grown (or developed) in faith so that which was unnatural can become natural. Even Jesus grew in wisdom and favor (Luke 2:52).

Paul speaks about power gifts in 1 Corinthians 12 (v8-12), which again, are for the common good and for the building up of the Body. Where the other gifts can be more personality-driven, these gifts are manifestations of the Holy Spirit. If you are pursuing these power gifts above the others, I want to suggest that your motives could be off. Maybe you want them for what they'll do or how they'll make you look. We need to make sure we are first "following the way of love" and being faithful. God has corrected me in this area before. But as we are faithful, willing recipients, let us "eagerly desire the greater gifts," and expect the Holy Spirit to give as He determines.

Later in 1 Corinthians 12, we see Paul mention gifts from all three of these sets and then some, showing that no list is all-inclusive, but common threads are clear. First, all gifts are for building up the Body, by preparing us to effectively serve. When God gifts you as a pastor or a musician, it can build you up, but it's primarily for the building of the Body. The gift of a prayer language appears to be the only exception, as it's for personal edification; however, you are building up yourself for the good of the whole. Second, gifts need to be developed, and those who are faithful are entrusted with more. God gives you a measure of faith. If you fan the flame, he gives you more faith. Don't stop fanning! May we "lack no spiritual gift as we eagerly wait for our Lord Jesus to be revealed" (1 Cor. 1:7).

Practically, you can discover your gifting as you pray through them like the fruit. "God, would you baptize me with the gift of ... Give me a measure of faith so I can do it. Help me to establish the character necessary to be entrusted with ..." If you are doing your part (faithfully developing your character), you can eagerly seek the Holy Spirit to do what only He can do. Let us be expectant as we trust Him to give as He determines.

As we are faithful, let us not neglect the practical steps. If we want the gift of healing, we need to pray for sick people. We must be diligent and give the Holy Spirit a platform to manifest Himself. As we practice, lay down our lives, allow the Holy Spirit to prune (particularly our motivation), and get God's heart, God will meet us with His anointing of power. It's our responsibility to fan the flame and develop the gifts of God. When we do, expect Holy Spirit to fulfill His role.

If we are only looking for tasks that
we can accomplish, we don't need God.

Life is difficult. We will face challenges. Many wish to have a little more time, but what we really need is more power. We need power for the task, not a task within our power. If we are only looking for tasks that we can accomplish, we don't need God. But God has created us to live life holding His hand and to accomplish tasks bigger than we can handle alone. This desire for impact and meaning is in each one of us. We need a transformation of perception.

God! Thank you for creating each of us with unique value. There are no step-kids in Heaven! Take us from our limited mindsets and usher us into our place as sons and daughters, a royal priesthood, who turn this world upside down.

Your dreams for us are so much larger than we can ask for or imagine. I declare my need for you to see your fullness come forth. Pour out your grace upon me to be faithful, to be willing, and to trust that you will empower me as I seek you. I trust you. I trust you. I am all in.

CHAPTER 8

From Heaven to Earth (The Power from on High)

If our heart's desire is to go *all in*, we need help. We cannot do it on our own. I know there are many different doctrinal beliefs about the Holy Spirit, but we can all agree on one thing. We need the power of God to do what He's called us to do.

In this chapter, I present a short succession of scriptures to give you an overview of events surrounding the start of Jesus' and the disciples' ministries as it relates to the power from on high. As we look at these scriptures and principles, we can clearly see what this power is and its purpose.

Before we focus on Jesus' ministry, let's start off with another member of the Godhead, the Holy Spirit. It's not easy to define who the Holy Spirit is, but let's look at how He has chosen to represent Himself.

Hovering—Genesis 1

Pillar of Fire and Smoke—Exodus 13

Resting temporarily upon special ones—Numbers 11

Jesus' baptism, receives indwelling—Matthew 3

Indwelling Believers—John 20

Power from on High—Acts 2

In the Old Testament, the Holy Spirit revealed Himself to the children of Israel as a pillar of fire (Ex. 13:21)—a huge, blazing blowtorch in the middle of the desert, large enough to be seen by thousands of people. It was a great wonder, a very impersonal wonder, which gave guidance. Its purpose was to give direction to the Israelites—when it moved, they moved.

by Diana Gaines

In the New Testament, the Holy Spirit also revealed Himself as fire, but much differently. The fire "separated and came to rest on each" of the disciples (Acts 2:3).

Do me a favor... You know the dainty, cupped-hand, Miss America wave? Ok. Do that wave quickly over your head. Don't worry, no one's looking. You're not allowed to read on until you do it...

In Acts 2, instead of one big flame, the Holy Spirit manifests himself as little "tongues of fire," just like your hand waving, over the disciples' heads. You can stop waving your hand now.

Wow. Fire over people's heads sounds cool, but what does it mean? God just set a new precedent for His followers. The Holy Spirit is no longer impersonal, but imparted, in fullness to individuals. This is the New Covenant. The Holy Spirit wants to abide in you, not just with you. God desires to reveal Himself and give you, His follower, direction and guidance. He wants to lead you on a journey from fear and paranoia to intimacy and power.

When we are anointed with fire, we are anointed to be the light of the world, a royal priesthood, sons and daughters of the Most High God. As we each walk in our anointing and work together in unity, we'll see the purposes of God become manifested. We'll see the fire get brighter.

Seeking Signs

In light of these two contrasting expressions of the Holy Spirit, it makes a little more sense why Jesus said to the religious leaders, "It's a wicked generation that seeks a sign" (Matt. 16:4). Have you ever wondered why He said that? Ever wonder if it applies to you? I know I want to see miraculous signs.

It's not that Jesus doesn't want us to see miracles or signs, but He knows the Father's heart. The Father doesn't want to speak to us only through miraculous signs. Jesus was focusing on something in particular with this statement. Let me give you a silly illustration.

What if I treated my wife like many of us treat God? What if I said to Diana, "Oh dear wife... Thank thee for thy dinner thy hands preparedest—I mean, thanks for cooking last night. Hey, when I come back from work, if you still love me, please light the two candles on the kitchen table. And, if you want me to take out the trash, blow one of them out. And hey, if you want to go to the movies, light a third candle."

It may sound cute, but if I relate to my wife like that, we wouldn't have a relationship. What I'm really saying is, "Diana, I don't want to talk to you or spend time with you. I don't want to be intimate. I just want to communicate through some distant, impersonal form of communication. Just give me a sign. I just want a sign."

Jesus was speaking words of life, the very words of the Father, but the Pharisees wouldn't push past their pride to listen. They were demanding a sign from heaven, even though miracles were performed and the Truth was right in front of them. They were more concerned with doing religion their way—the old, impersonal way—than truly connecting with God.

That's why God is grieved by a generation who seeks signs. They'd rather have signs than seek Him. God talks to unbelievers through signs, prophets, and other people (even through you and me), but He doesn't want that to be the primary way He speaks to His children. He wants to speak to us through direct access. The open communion with God, which was lost in the Garden of Eden, was reinstated through the life, death, and resurrection of Jesus Christ. He gave his life so He could speak to you with a still, small voice. It is wicked to ignore all that Christ did, not to mention God's heart for relationship, and demand impersonal blessing and guidance.

Jesus Anointed by the Holy Spirit

God's desire is for close relationship. He wants to dwell within us, and the Bible tells us why. Before Jesus starts His public ministry, John the

Baptizer prepares the way. Each gospel records John saying, "I baptize you with water for repentance. But after me will come one who is more powerful than I... He will baptize you with the Holy Spirit and with fire." (Matt. 3:11, Luke 3:16, Mark 1:8, John 1: 26-33. The Mark verse doesn't include every word and the John section includes more words.)

The Bible tends to repeat concepts that are important. It's like God saying, "You need to get this!" If all the gospels say something, it's probably something God really wants us to understand. So, just to clarify, John is baptizing with water for repentance. One is coming after him who will baptize with the Holy Spirit and fire for... It doesn't say, but John 1 tells us who. God told John, "The man on you see the Spirit come down on and remain is the One (who will baptize with the Holy Spirit)" (John 1:33).

Here's how it happens in Matthew 3... John is preaching with the spirit of conviction and lots of people are getting baptized in the Jordan River. Why? Baptism is a public proclamation of an eternal change of heart. It signifies that sin is washed down the river and those exiting the water are purified. Many people are realizing they are sinners, and they want to get right with God. They want to make a public statement, so John the Baptizer baptized.

One day, John is in the Jordan River baptizing with water for repentance. Out of the crowd of tax collectors, soldiers, Pharisees, and prostitutes walks Jesus. It probably went something like this:

(Splash)

John: (to self) "Wow, that last guy was heavy..."

(to the crowd) "Ok, who's next? Oh! Hey... Jesus?"

(to self) "Huh? I thought he was the One. What about those prophecies spoken over our lives before we were born? Why is he coming to me? Doesn't he know I'm baptizing for repentance? Is he saying he's a sinner...?"

Jesus: "Hey Cuz." (They were cousins you know)

John: "Umm... I should be baptized by you? Why are you coming to me? I don't understand..."

Jesus: "Let it be so now," *wink, wink* " You know, to fulfill all righteousness."

John: "Well, I guess... In the name of the..."

(Splash—KAWOOOSH!)

As soon as Jesus comes up out of the water, the rest of the Trinity shows up. The heavens open, the Holy Spirit comes down like a lightning dove, and the Father cheers like a dad at his kid's little league game: "That's my boy! I'm so proud of Him!"

When God shows up, He's not too concerned about keeping our little theological boxes intact. He can make a mess of things. He acts like He's God or something. He acts like He owns everything and everyone and doesn't need to be confined by the way we think things should work.

I'm pretty sure that John never expected he'd baptize God. I mean, why would he? If "The One" got baptized, doesn't that mean He's repenting? John's baptism was for repentance. But if "The One" is repenting, that means He sinned, right? Or maybe, like in many other situations, Jesus was showing us the perfect example.

Jesus made Himself nothing. Though He was by very nature God, He took on human likeness, not just in appearance. When Jesus came to earth, He had no power in Himself (Phil. 2:5-8). In fact, up until the incredible moment when the Trinity had a family reunion, Jesus had a self-life. It was not a selfish life, because He didn't sin, but a self-life where His concerns were a family, a home, and running the family business. He didn't have a ministry or perform any miracles up to that point. He walked into the Jordan River on the Israeli side with a self-life and powerless. Jesus was baptized, which signified His self-life being washed away, and received the power from on high. He then walked out on the Jordanian desert side of the river washed of his self-life and filled with the Holy Spirit. From that moment forth, He only did what He saw His Father doing. He received the power from on high to walk in the fullness of His calling (a good summary is found in Isaiah 61).

I'd like to point out a couple of things that may be really obvious. God is really smart. He knew Jesus needed a powerful anointing to fulfill His calling. Also, Jesus knew that to the extent He surrendered Himself, the Holy Spirit could fill Him. And to the extent He surrendered His will, the Father could show Him what to do. Likewise, with us, God will anoint us proportional to our callings. To the extent that you say yes to God and surrender your will, is to that extent that God's anointing pours out.

God doesn't anoint you just so you can feel good or have a title. He wants to build up His people. Your willingness to minister to His people will determine His willingness to give you the power from on high to minister. To the degree that you give up your life, you'll save it, and to the degree you try to save your life, you'll lose it (Matt. 10:39).

Jesus never performed miracles with a power from within Himself (remember Phil. 2:5-8). He performed miracles because He was obedient to His Father and anointed by the Holy Spirit. No one goes into the river sinless like Jesus and if we think we can do things for God without His anointing, we are gravely mistaken. If Jesus needed the power, we need it that much more.

The Disciples and the Holy Spirit

Now, let's move on to the disciples. Before we get the power from on high part, let's fill in some background. In the book of John, after the last supper, Jesus shares his last words with his disciples. John chapters 13-17 is one of the most important passages in the whole Bible. They are Jesus' last words, and He describes in detail the ministry of the Holy Spirit in the life of a believer. Jesus explains He is about to die, but He will ask the Father to send another Counselor. He then says, the Counselor (the Holy Spirit), will not only live with them but will be in them. Jesus is about to clear the way for God to reinstate what was wrecked in Genesis.

Jesus also prophesies that all His disciples will fall away (Matt. 26, Mark 14). Not the most encouraging prophesy, huh? Peter, being the passionate, impulsive person he was, replies, "Even if all fall away, I never will." Apparently, Peter didn't fully understand the word *all*. To be fair, I think many of us have done that at an altar call. "I'm passionate for you Lord, I'll do anything..." Peter was set up for such an intense failure because God wanted to raise him up as a great leader.

It's like being a Race Car Driver. You can't be a good one until you've crashed some cars. It's called 11/10ths driving. You actually lose control, but not so bad as you can't regain it. You don't truly find that limit (or right over it) until you hit the wall—and maybe spend some time in reconstructive surgery. But when you come back, you can push it to the edge, but back off a touch. Your greatest advancements in life often coincide with your greatest failures. It's when you fall down and fail, you realize your limitations and how much you need God.

Just a few hours later, Jesus' last supper words are fulfilled. He is killed and all his disciples abandon Him. Passionate, impulsive, prideful Peter denies Jesus three times and is completely broken. He crashes, which is extremely vital in preparation for the power from on high. But for now, things are looking pretty bad.

Let's pick up the scene in John 20, three days after the crucifixion. The disciples aren't doing too well. They're all together, and they're scared. So scared in fact, that all the doors are locked. The last three years had been great, but all for nothing. They gave up everything for the One who they thought would redeem Israel, but He was just brutally executed. Who's next? Not only that, but Jesus' body went missing earlier that day. Was His body stolen? Was He alive? So many questions.

All of a sudden, a ghost shows up! The disciples scream. Maybe one even peed in his pants or said a bad word. "OH ****!" It's Jesus standing with them, and he says the best thing to say to people scared out of their minds: "Peace be with you." The disciples saw and rejoiced. They became the very first New Testament converts (they believed and confessed (Rom. 10:9-10)). Jesus breathed on them, and they received the Holy Spirit. The disciples received the peace of God and could enjoy a relationship with God not experienced since the Garden of Eden. On top of that, they were cleansed from sin and joined a royal priesthood, not by man's appointment, but the Lord's.

If you were one of those disciples, what would you have done? In light of all they just witnessed and now filled with the Holy Spirit, don't you think they'd shout it from the rooftops? They should've kicked down the door shouting, "Jerusalem! He's alive! Jesus of Nazareth, whom you crucified. HE'S ALIVE!" None of them did any of that. Why? The disciples received the peace of God, but not the power to do His bidding. They knew they were sons, but they were not yet empowered to be ambassadors. They were saved, they had the Holy Spirit, yet they were still missing something.

But wait, they had the Holy Spirit. They're saved. What more do they need? With salvation, don't you get the Holy Spirit according to the New Testament? Yes. Don't you get everything you need? No, you don't. Many Christians are saved but lack the power to stand up for Christ.

How about you? Maybe you were baptized with water for repentance, but never experienced the baptism of fire. You may have the assurance of salvation and a relationship with God, but you're a wimp and have no power or ability to overcome sin in your life. You certainly don't have the boldness and the ability to be the representative of Christ that God wants you to be on the face of this earth.

If this is the case, you are no different than the disciples at this point. They were in the upper room where they received the peace of God and had the Holy Spirit dwelling within them. They were saved, just saw the risen Christ, and then... they went home. Not only did they go back to Galilee, but they went back to what they did before they met Jesus. They were saved, they had the Holy Spirit, and they went fishing (John 21:3).

There is some very important insight in this story. Peter, a leader among the disciples, decides to go back to fishing and take half of the crew with him. As the story goes, these experienced fishermen end up fishing all night without a catch. As day breaks, a stranger on shore appears. They see Jesus, but they don't recognize it's Him. There are so many times in life that we are looking straight at Jesus and don't realize it's Him.

"Children!" He shouts, "Haven't you caught any fish?" Wow, I can't think of a better way to annoy professional fishermen. But Jesus can, he's cooking up some fish for breakfast. A normally hotheaded Peter probably would have said some bad words. Instead, he simply answers, "No. No fish."

As if the former instigations weren't enough, the stranger yells, "Throw the net on the other side of the boat!" In the beginning of the gospels, when Jesus said something similar, Peter responded in a way to preserve his dignity. This time, though he was called a child, probably smells sizzling fish, and told to do something pretty pointless, he simply obeys. Peter and the disciples are broken. Brokenness brings forth humility.

When they obey, they haul in the catch of a lifetime and realize that the stranger is Jesus. Peter is so excited he gets dressed and swims to shore. Back on shore, Jesus reaffirms, redeems, and reminds Peter of the calling on his life. Peter's brokenness was preparing him for Pentecost.

There is an incredible call on Peter's life, one that can't be accomplished without the power and anointing of God. Remember what I said about Jesus' call and anointing? To the extent He surrendered Himself, the Holy Spirit could fill Him. And to the extent He surrendered His will, the Father's will could be done. Unless Peter was broken of himself and his strong will, he could not accomplish God's will for His life. So, it is with us. If you don't want to yield yourself and are just looking for a task you are able to do, you are trying to do something without God. You want to set up your life so you don't need Him. On the other hand, if you want to walk in the supernatural promises of God and fulfill His purposes on this earth you must submit. You need to lay down yourself and go all in.

Let's jump forward to Acts 1. At this point, Jesus had appeared to his disciples over a period of 40 days. They had the peace of the Holy Spirit, were abiding with God but weren't doing anything about it. Right before He ascended, Jesus gathered His followers together and commanded them to not leave Jerusalem but wait for what the Father had promised. Referring back to what John the Baptizer prophesied, he then promises: "For John baptized with water, but you will be baptized with the Holy Spirit." Before He goes, He tells them the purpose of that baptism: "You will receive the power of Holy Spirit and will be my witnesses in Jerusalem... and to the ends of the earth."

There it is, clear as day, in the words of Jesus Himself. The purpose of the power from on high is the anointing, the enabling, the power to be His witnesses.

Ten days later, they were all together and it happened. Well, 120 were there. Even though Jesus appeared to 500 people (1 Cor. 15:6), only 120 were in the upper room. Where were the rest? Did they get tired of waiting? It was only ten days later, but no one knew how long it would take. Jesus didn't give a date. Did the rest of the 500 just not get the invitation or did they decide they waited long enough? Maybe they gave up. Maybe they wanted to do ministry in their own strength. God is faithful. He always fulfills His promises. We need to stay hungry for the Lord and stand firm in faith. Whatever the circumstances were for the other 380 in Acts 2, they missed something big.

Here's what happened. The sound of a violent wind filled the house. Tongues of fire separated and fell on each one. Go ahead and wave your hand over your head again. There was fire resting on their heads (like your hand) and they were FILLED with the Holy Spirit, the power from on high. So, what did it do? Well, let's see what happens next.

First, they began to speak in other languages. Why? That was the gift that was needed. Jews from all over (15 places are mentioned v.9-12) were in Jerusalem to celebrate the Feast of Pentecost. Anointed by the Holy Spirit, the disciples were preaching the gospel in the visitors' native tongues. In His wisdom, the Holy Spirit gave the supernatural gifts that were necessary to build the body.

Second, Peter was given courage (v. 14), the boldness to be a witness. This man, who denied Christ three times out of fear, all of a sudden had the audacity to proclaim a message that would surely rile people up and maybe get him killed. "JERUSALEM! Jesus, whom you crucified! HE'S ALIVE!"

by David Dew

Peter was transformed from a wimp to a guy with a death wish, or one not afraid to die. This empowerment to be a witness, this boldness, is another evidence of the baptism of the Holy Spirit.

Third, Peter was given divine illumination. The Spirit empowered Peter to speak, tie scriptures together, and give instruction (repent, water baptism, and receive power). It was one of the greatest sermons of all time. Three thousand people got saved!

There are other evidences of the baptism of the Holy Spirit (including the power to impart saving impressions on men, to prevail, to teach and anoint, to work miracles, to lay hands on others—so they may receive power from on high, to exercise gifts, to live sacrificial, cross-bearing life, of great meekness, of loving enthusiasm, of loving and living faith, to endure great persecution, and to be martyrs) which the disciples displayed in the book of Acts and beyond. All the evidences have this in common: they empower us to be witnesses of Christ. That is the purpose of the power.

The purpose of the power from on high is to empower us to be witnesses of Christ.

When it comes to the power from on high, different doctrines claim different things that I don't believe are biblical. I want to address a few of them. One thought is that the gifts are not for today; there is a separation between the Gospels and Acts, and the Epistles. In the time of Jesus and the book of Acts, God poured out in a special way to build the church. But now, God has done away with that pattern and gave the Epistles to build our church on today. The error in this doctrine is most Epistles were written in the same time frame that Acts was taking place, which means **there is no such separation**. Man created this doctrine as a response to personal experience (or lack thereof) instead of what the Word actually says.

Another claims that the primary evidence of the baptism of the Holy Spirit is speaking in tongues, and if that gift is not present, neither is the power from on high. I don't want to diminish the power and importance of a prayer language but speaking in tongues is of little importance if we are not being witnesses of Christ. One of the most anointed men I've ever known, Gordon Olson, never spoke in tongues. The primary evidence is that you're in love with God and you are bringing people into right relationship with Him. The first gift was tongues because that's the gift that was needed. The primary evidence of the power from on high must be whether or not we are being those fruitful witnesses of our powerful, loving God.

Another common thought is skepticism towards "Charismatic stuff." They resist the gifts of God because they've observed Charismatic Christians without character. Let me tell you what, I've known many people that got saved and abused salvation. Should I reject salvation? It's the same with the gifts.

The final common mindset I want to address is people who say they need to be right with the Lord before they get baptized in the Holy Spirit. Though developing our character is important, we don't have to be perfect before we receive salvation. When we are in relationship with God, He walks with us and helps us throughout the process. It's the same way with the baptism of the Holy Spirit. God doesn't baptize people because of their character. He baptizes us with His fire because He loves us. When we say yes to the Great Commission, He wants to empower us through the Holy Spirit to live lives that represent Him.

Whether you are familiar with these paradigms or not, I hope that this chapter and deeper study into the word will help form a Biblical worldview of the power from on high and its importance in our lives. If Jesus needed the power to accomplish God's will for His time on earth, how much more do we? If we are going to be accurate representations of our awesome God, we need to be empowered and inspired by His Spirit.

Here at the close of this chapter, let's be honest with ourselves. What's the status of your relationship with God?

Maybe you know a lot about God, but you never met Him. You prayed a prayer, but this relationship is not active in your heart. You cannot have a casual relationship with the King of kings. If you haven't been totally revolutionized by your meeting God, then you need to meet Him in a new way.

It's possible you are like the disciples in that upper room (in John 20), seeing the resurrected Christ for the first time. You believe and have confidence you are a child of God and the peace of the Holy Spirit. And though you have assurance, you're aware of your lack of empowerment. You have the peace, but lack the power, and feel a bit like a wimp when it comes to being a witness.

Maybe you've been empowered and have been a witness of Christ through word and action. Awesome. Paul admonishes us in 1 Cor. 12:31, to "eagerly desire the greater gifts." God wants to give good gifts to His kids and there is no end to His generosity. All throughout the book of Acts, the disciples ask for more, and God is faithful to pour out more.

If you've decided to go all in, it doesn't matter where you are. Let's go boldly into the throne room and ask Him for more! Lord, we want to be filled with more of Your glory!

As His son or daughter let's each ask for each of these gifts on the following page to be an extension of His love whenever needed. Pray through each one of these gifts and ask God to bring to remembrance and empower us with authority whenever the opportunity arises.

These things shall follow those who believe...

The power of/to:

1. Speak in Tounges
2. Moral courage & boldness
3. Divine illumination
4. Impart saving impressions
5. Prevail with God & man
6. Teaching with anointing
7. Work miracles
8. Gift of inspiration
9. Impart power from on high
10. Exercise variety of gifts
11. Live a self-sacrificing life
12. Live a cross-bearing life
13. Exercise great meekness
14. Loving enthusiasm for Christ
15. Great discernment of spirits
16. Loving & living faith
17. Overcome self-centeredness
18. Endure great wisdom
19. Administer words of knowledge
20. Interpret Tounges
21. Impart life-giving encouragement
22. Commission others into ministry

Pray to receive each one of these for His glory!

by Kip Gaines

CHAPTER 9

Three Origins of Thought (Fear vs Faith)

God designed humans for a direct access relationship with Himself. When Adam and Eve chose to rebel, God didn't come up with a Plan B. Instead, He wants His highest to be realized, so He made a way for Plan A to be reinstated. That's why Jesus came. Jesus' life, death, and resurrection made direct access possible once again. Though direct access is now possible, because we live in a world of five influences, we also need discernment. Even within our own minds we have conflicting thoughts. Here are the three origins of our thoughts: our own thoughts, God inspired thoughts (through direct access), and the adversary inspired thoughts. Let's take a deeper look at these three origins and what accompanies them.

Though many scriptures display the three origins of thought, one scene in the gospels clearly shows all three. In Matthew 16, Jesus and his disciples are on a stroll and Jesus asks, "Who do people say that I am?"

The disciples start spouting off what others say, because, well, it's ok if other people are wrong. "Some say John the Baptist."

"Some say Elijah."

"I've heard one of the other prophets."

Then Jesus cuts to the heart and asks, "Who do you say that I am?"

The disciples look sheepishly at each other, and then they start looking at the one who usually puts his foot in his mouth. Cue Simon (Peter).

Simon clears his throat and answers, "You are the Christ, the Son of the living God." He was certainly not ready for the reaction he was about to receive.

Jesus answers, "WOOOOOAAAHH!! Blessed are you Simon, son of Jonah!, for flesh and blood has not revealed this to you, but My Father who is in heaven!" Jesus is impressed. I imagine Simon blushing a little and walking a little taller. Jesus just told him that he, Simon, heard from God. This event is so monumental, that Jesus decides to mark this occasion by changing Simon's name to Peter, meaning rock. Jesus then declares that Peter's revelation is the very foundation of every New Testament believer, "...and on this rock, I will build my church" (v. 18). The revelation that Jesus is Messiah, THE Savior, is the foundation of the church. There never was and never will be another savior.

Peter (aka Simon) has this incredible revelation from God which is the very foundation of the church. Not only that, but he received a new name to mark this moment. Jesus then commands the disciples to keep that revelation on the down low and begins to open up about the plan to save the world. "Yes, it's true, but we need to keep it hush-hush. Listen fellas, I'll let you in on the plan. We are going back to Jerusalem. Yeah, I know the religious leaders don't like me and want to kill me, but listen. This is hard to understand, but I am going to suffer, be killed, and then I will rise again."

Peter, who is feeling pretty good about himself now that he has heard from God and all, assumes he should use his supreme wisdom and defuse the situation. After all, a leader predicting his own death isn't too good for morale. So Peter, being the rock that he is, takes Jesus aside and rebukes Him, "Never Jesus! C'mon, this will never happen..."

Jesus cuts him off, "GET BEHIND ME, SATAN!"

Now, it's never a good idea to rebuke God. Peter was definitely in over his head. But let's put ourselves in Peters sandals. Could you imagine hearing that phrase during your quiet time? "Get behind me Satan." Not the most affirming. Now, Jesus isn't giving Simon Peter another name. Peter's newest 'revelation,' that Jesus shouldn't be talking about own His death, was averse to the will of God and Jesus called him out.

What do you do when you hear voices contrary to God's? We need to do the exact same thing Jesus did. Before we get into that, let's recount Peter's wild rollercoaster ride. He went from generally bewildered disciple to the rock (who officially hears from God) to Satan. Wow, what a ride! Peter shows how easy it is to have your thoughts, then a God thought, then a devil thought. Not only are there separate origins sending different messages, but thoughts can happen so fast they can easily get mixed together. Obviously, this can be a problem for numerous reasons. For one, we can have an issue like Peter. We can totally hear from the Lord, feel great as we walk out in faith, and then listen to an adversarial thought contrary to God's will and be totally off.

These issues can easily arise when people claim to have the word of the Lord. In reality, only God has the pure word of the Lord. If God speaks to me, at best, I have the word of the Lord and Kip. The word is always influenced by both parties, and we work together as a team. The word can be anointed, but it has the flavor of its channel, container, messenger. This is evident in the books of the prophets; especially, where different prophets reflect God's character differently in their prophecies. That's how it's designed, and we need to keep this in mind when giving or receiving words.

How can we possibly navigate the intertwined mess of thoughts? Luckily, Paul helps us out in Romans 12:1-2.

> *Therefore, I urge you, brothers and sisters, in view of God's mercy, to offer your bodies as a living sacrifice, holy and pleasing to God—this is your true and proper worship. Do not conform to the pattern of this world but be transformed by the renewing of your mind. Then you will be able to test and approve what God's will is—His good, pleasing, and perfect will.*

This verse is pretty straightforward, but I want to point out a few things. First, as a sacrifice, should we be exerting our will? No, sacrifices are completely devoted to God. The more we lay down our wills, as a living sacrifice, the quieter our fleshly thoughts become. Second, what's the pattern of this world? This world promotes selfishness, chaos. and makes us think we know better than God. We are not designed to conform to that. When we accept Jesus as Lord, He pours out His grace and makes us a new creation (2 Cor. 5:17). As new creations we can not only hear God but can grow to test and approve what is of God and what is not (Rom 12:2).

Understanding the Origin of a Thought

So, how do we test and approve? "Well, I feel like this is..." No, emotions can be tricky. I'm sure Peter felt like he was doing the right thing by rebuking Jesus. Let's dig deeper. How can we understand the origin of a thought? We need wisdom gained through discernment. It's the nature of a thought that reveals its origin. Remember the ultimate intent chapter? It's the same basic pattern. We can make decisions that seem good but are really motivated by selfishness. These won't build God's kingdom or bear lasting fruit. Even if a thought feels right, we need to discern its nature and the end it's trying to secure.

This discerning process is very practical. First, we must develop an ear to hear what the Lord is speaking. All of creation testifies to the glory of God (Rom. 1), but most people don't want to listen. Next, we need to tune into the Spirit's frequency. This seems abstract, but it naturally occurs as we get to know God more (Mark 4:9; Rev 2:7).

In YWAM, we had this gym where we'd hold weekly worship services, etc. and it would get so noisy. But you know what? If my wife called my name from across the gym, I could hear it through the noise. I know Diana's voice because I know Diana. It may sound strange, but this is normally called selective listening or discernment. This ability allows me to hear the frequency of her voice through all the other static. The more we read the Word and spend time with God, the clearer we'll hear that still, small voice through the static of life.

Finally, after listening and discerning, we need wisdom. Wisdom is the ability to act on our discernment. Wisdom allows us to process the voice of God and His nature through the truth of His Word (the Bible) and know what we are to do. Using wisdom, we can understand the end our thought is trying to secure (its ultimate intent) and determine its true origin.

Just like the Israelites, we are called to "harken unto the voice of Lord…" (Deut. 28:1). The word *harken* in the King James is *shama* in Hebrew, which means to listen and obey. To listen is to have faith, "Faith comes by hearing," (Rom. 10:17) and to obey is to live a lifestyle of repentance. To have faith and walk in repentance (to listen and obey) is how we live in this salvation relationship.

Peter thought he was doing the right thing by rebuking Jesus. "Come on Jesus, don't say stuff like that." But Jesus knew what was right, God's good, pleasing, and perfect will. Peter's thought, whether originating from his flesh or the adversary, was not lined up with the word of God. Therefore, Peter's rebuke needed to be called out for what it was—adverse to God's will. Jesus couldn't allow him to bring confusion to the rest of the disciples.

Before we move on to another facet of this, let's recap. There are three origins of thought: the flesh (ourselves), God, and the adversary. A thought's origin is evident through its nature, which can be discerned. The only way to develop that discernment and have wisdom is by holding God's hand and growing in the understanding of His nature as seen through reading His love letters (the Bible).

Faith vs Fear vs Fear-Faith

With this understanding of the three origins of thought fresh on our minds, let's look at a much more common topic: faith. Faith is another concept that Christians have a hard time really grasping because they get caught up in specifics and try to make it fit their personal worldview. To more easily understand how faith fits into the Biblical worldview, we must compare it to its opposite (fear) and its counterfeit (fear-faith).

First of all, faith is aligned with God's thoughts. Simply put, faith is having God's thoughts and agreeing with them. Agreement can be as simple as a prayer or an act of obedience. Faith can always overcome fear because faith establishes the Kingdom of God. The journey or process of faith can bring a temporary death (death to self), but the end is always life. Fear and fear-faith, on the other hand, come from ourselves or the enemy.

Now each of these have something in common; they all project into the future. All three of these, faith, fear-faith, and fear, prophetically speak destiny into your life. Whichever you choose to focus on reveals the ultimate intention of your heart and determines the direction of your life.

Faith speaks life-filled destiny because it originates from God. Jeremiah 29:11 says: "I know the plans I have for you. Plans to prosper you and not to harm you, plans to give you a hope and a future." When you have faith, you have belief, encouragement, conviction, forgiveness, worth, acceptance, unity within the Body of Christ, humility, self-acceptance, trust, and embrace God's purposes. If faith confronts fear-faith of a religious spirit, division may occur, but true life is always secured. Jesus promises us that we will have tribulation in this world but remember He has overcome.

Fear-faith comes from the law without the Spirit and usually originates from our own thoughts. We walk in fear-faith when our obedience is motivated by a fear of consequences and not love. Fear-faith can come through religion, the law, performance, accusation, and codependency. If you are living bound up by religious laws and traditions, you live in fear-faith. If you are living for the acceptance and love of a spiritual leader, parent, or anyone else, you are living in fear-faith.

This prophetic voice causes you to be something or someone you are not. Fear-faith causes identity theft. First, you steal from yourself. You don't believe your true identity is good enough, so you take another role to become someone better. Oftentimes, through comparison we try to assume the role of another, stealing their identity. This leads to a performance orientation, forcing us to always show others an ideal self because we are afraid our true selves will fail.

Now, fear is having thoughts that are in agreement with Lucifer. It can be a spirit and doesn't require a rational cause. We can wake up in the middle of the night fearful for no reason. Fear is accompanied by accusation, doubt, condemnation, unworthiness, perfectionism, and distrust of God, self, others, etc. Basically, fear brings all that is opposite of what faith brings. It is the breeding ground for failure and isolation. When this is the origin of your thought, call it out! If fear is motivating your decision, IT'S

NOT FROM GOD! God has not given us a spirit of fear (2 Tim. 1:7).

Today, fear is on a global, worldwide attack. Terrorism is fueled by fear. Fear of pandemics has caused great harm. The jackhammer thought behind fear is: "I'm not safe. I'm not safe. I'm not safe." This is an anti-Christ thought. Of course, when threats abound, it makes sense where this thought comes from, but don't focus on this crazy world. Even if we die, "Oh death, where is your sting?" (1 Cor. 15:55). We have eternal security.

But, if you nurse the "I'm not safe" thought of fear, you eventually get angry. The jackhammer thought behind anger is, "I've been wronged. I've been wronged." After this anger is nursed, it often shifts into lust: "I deserve because I've been wronged." Here you demand whatever because you're a victim and you've been wronged. This lust easily justifies behavior that is inconsistent with the purpose for which you were created. In this progression, we align ourselves with things like accusation, self-pity, performance, or other things that come from fear. We end up distrusting God, others, and ourselves. If you are constantly battling a spirit of fear or stuck in a fear-faith mentality, you need to be anointed with a greater understanding of the Father's love. You are His son or daughter.

Faith, on the other hand, results in rest. In Hebrews 4, Paul talks about those who believe "enter into rest." Do something for me real quick. Stop reading for a moment and take a deep breath. Ok, now let it out. Rest. Nice, huh? Paul knew what he was talking about. But wait... Paul? How insanely busy was that guy? How can he say he entered in rest? When you read Acts and his letters, it doesn't seem that Paul did too much resting.

We typically think that rest is not doing anything. But when you do things of, from, or to yourself and the source is you, it's not faith. It's not true rest. Whenever you make decisions motivated by fear, there's no rest. True rest in the soul, even in the midst of life's busyness, is only felt when you obey and commune with God. It's when we walk in *shalom*, God's divine order. This is the abiding that Jesus talks about in John 15. We can rest because we go to God with everything and it's all, ultimately, on Him.

God shows us how to filter our thoughts (Phil. 4:8) to live in rest. This isn't just a nice idea but the strategy for overcoming fear and sin. If we keep our minds focused on "whatever is good, whatever is pure," we **will** overcome fear and enter into rest.

Jesus only did what He saw the Father do. He always lived in faith and was never motivated by fear—not even while facing the cross. There's no record of Jesus walking in fear-faith trying to win the Father's acceptance. Jesus knew He was loved; His Father spoke it from heaven. He was at peace in the midst of joy, grief, sorrow, or pain.

I've heard it preached that Jesus took all of our sorrow and grief, so we don't need to experience it. Nothing is further from the truth. He went before us to show us how to walk in it rightly. He didn't go to the cross so we wouldn't have to, He showed us how. Jesus was baptized in the Holy Spirit to show us how. I could go on, but you get the idea.

Jesus showed us how we were created to live. We were designed to live lives of faith, with direct access trusting our Father, and establishing the Kingdom of God on earth with Him. We build the kingdom of God by living in the image and likeness of God, responding to conviction, loving God and others, bringing forth God's will on the face of the earth, and looking forward to the fulness of His promises. Obeying God, going *all in*, is the only way we can truly walk in victory and rest.

As Christians, we should be building the kingdom of God, but is that always true? When we live in fear and that fear motivates our decisions, what kingdom are we building? What if we are motivated by fear-faith? Ever hear (or make) statements like these? "Well, I'm building the Kingdom of God because I said the prayer."

"Seriously, I go to church every Sunday and go on outreaches."

"I must be building the Kingdom because I'm a pastor/ missionary."

Remember the Ultimate Intent of the Heart chapter? Our outward acts are not as important as our motivations. We make the choice whether or not to live in faith every day. When we live in fear or fear faith, even in ignorance, we build up the Kingdom of Darkness.

Conviction vs Condemnation

This difference becomes clear when we respond to guilt. In essence, guilt is to our spirits what pain is to our bodies. It's a warning that something is out of alignment. Guilt can be helpful or destructive, depending on whether it takes the form of conviction or condemnation. Conviction is from God while condemnation is from the enemy, others, or yourself. So, how do we know? Again, we need to look at the nature of the guilt and what end is it trying to secure.

Conviction is good and originates from God or yourself. When you respond to it, you feel greater value and freedom. Conviction is the surgical knife that purges us of our carnality and conforms us into the image of Christ. To the degree we respond to the conviction of the Holy Spirit in our life is to the degree we will be conformed into the image of Christ. When we resist conviction, it often becomes condemnation.

Condemnation is not good. It occurs when the guilt is unclear, causing confusion and feelings of insignificance. When you respond to it, you feel less valuable and become more confused. Condemnation often aligns itself with fear and causes us to act more out of the fear of punishment than the joy of faithful obedience. These fearful thoughts usually originate from the enemy, often after we resist conviction. To the degree we reject the conviction of the Holy Spirit is to the degree that we will be conformed into the image of Lucifer.

Whether you call yourself a Christian or not, how we process guilt reveals if we are really walking in faith or not. What do you do when guilt arises? If you live in fear or fear-faith, you really think like a humanist. That means your purpose, the end of all being, is your own happiness. When you recognize guilt, you want that discomfort to go away. Guilt doesn't make you happy. You need to get rid of guilt so you can be happy again. 'Christian humanists' go to God and ask for forgiveness while other humanists do a good deed (or something) to tip the karma balance. In either case, this is done primarily to relieve the guilt. Why? To feel happy again, of course. Our purpose for living is fulfilled. We are happy. Then life as usual continues, until ugh... I don't feel happy anymore. I know! I can ask for forgiveness again and get relief from this guilt. "GOD! I'm sorry, I'll never do it again. Please forgive me so I can be happy again." Can you see a cycle forming?

> *To the degree we respond to the conviction of the*
> *Holy Spirit in our life is to the degree we will be*
> *conformed into the image of Christ.*

So many 'Christians' are stuck living in this cycle. Most of the time they want to be free from their sin, but they never experience true freedom. Why? Because the ultimate intention of their heart is incorrect; the end of all being is not the happiness of man. That's not the purpose of our lives. As long as we are living for our own happiness, God is simply an errand boy with whom to bargain. We want God to compromise His standards so we can live how we want to live, but it doesn't work that way. As Christians, we are required to live by faith. By faith you have been saved (Eph. 2:8). Without faith it is impossible to please God (Heb. 11:6). Only a life of faith leads to freedom. If you are in bondage to sin, at best you are walking in fear faith and you are listening to the wrong voice.

If this is hitting you hard right now, it's not condemnation. Cut it out! Quit living for your own happiness. God has a better deal for you, a greater purpose for your life. He wants you to live in true, real freedom.

He desires to pour out all his love, joy, peace, power, etc. into you. He wants to be in unity with each one of us and all He asks for in return is that we would share all of us with Him. "He who desires to save His life, will lose it. But he who lays down his life will gain it" (Matt. 10:39). He who focuses on his own happiness will never find it. God wants to share His fullness with us if we'd only give Him all of our lives which (by the way) is way less. This unfair deal is the desire of heaven.

When you experience guilt and you're kingdom-minded (walking in faith), you ask for forgiveness for the purpose of victory. Yeah, it doesn't feel good, but you respond because your victory establishes the Kingdom of God. This does make you happy, but your focus is the victory and glory of God. After you're forgiven, you then can ask to be anointed and empowered by the Holy Spirit to continually walk in this victory. As you do, you share that victory with others which further builds the kingdom of God. In faith, we don't live for God's, others', or our own happiness alone, but all occur when we align ourselves with His purposes. This is the most fulfilling, rewarding, incredible end that you can possibly secure.

There are times I don't like conviction. Sometimes I run from or push it away because I want to do whatever I wanted. My purpose for living, the end of all being, was the happiness of Kip. Sometimes that meant doing things that didn't glorify God. Sometimes it meant asking for forgiveness just to relieve the guilt. I let my heart get hardened, so sin was more natural than righteousness and I didn't care about building the Kingdom of God. Thank God that He calls me out and continues to re-sensitize my heart as I respond to His conviction. Now I welcome conviction. Conviction, when embraced, allows me to be transformed into the image of Jesus.

So, which kingdom are you building? What prophetic voice are you listening to? If you want to be part of establishing the kingdom of God, you must get to know who God is and receive who He has called you to be. Are you willing?

Lord, I am willing. I receive your conviction. I want to go all in and be transformed into the image of Jesus. Help me discern the origins of my thoughts. I want to walk in faith and in the calling you have for my life.

CHAPTER 10

6,000 Years
and Still *All In*

Have you come to a moment of decision? Even Jesus had a moment like this. Yes, He was always completely God and completely human, making Him completely different from every other human. However, He was not always in the public spotlight. There was a moment He was faced with a choice, and if he agreed there would be no turning back.

Shortly, after Jesus was baptized in the Jordan River by his cousin John, His mother asked him to fix a problem. "Son, the wedding is in trouble. The wine has run out and we need to continue the celebration" (John 2).

Jesus knew if he performed a public miracle, he would publicly reveal his identity. Once this happened, there would be no turning back. He responds, "My hour has not yet come." We're not sure what kind of mother and son looks went back and forth, but Mary seems to ignore her son. She tells the servants to do whatever Jesus says to do. You know the rest of the story, water becomes wine. He performs a public miracle. The transition happens. He reveals Himself for who He really is! He's *all in* and there's no turning back.

Lord give us this resolve to make, like you, a public declaration where there is no turning back.

Jesus is our example, but remember, He is a perfect reflection of the Father. We need to understand that God has been all in with mankind for over 6000 years! Let's start at the beginning.

2,000 years from Adam to Abraham

In Genesis 1, God creates the heavens and the earth. Then God creates humans: "Let us make man in our image, in our likeness..." (1:26). Remember, that doesn't mean we're made out of God stuff. We are not created to be Him but like Him. He created us to be in relationship and do with our stuff in miniature what He does with His stuff in magnitude.

Man was given authority over the earth, and in the cool of the evening Adam and Eve had direct access. They walked with God, and it was AWESOME. But sadly, Adam and Eve wanted to be like God, instead of trusting Him. They wanted their will to be done and they broke perfect relationship. **The curse of sin entered the world, but God always has a plan to restore.**

In the following chapters, it appears most men decided not to relate with their Heavenly Father. Though a few walked with God (like Enoch) (Gen. 5:24), things got so bad by Genesis 6 the Lord decided to start over with Noah (Gen. 6:13). Unfortunately, it doesn't take long for Noah's descendants to stop trusting God. In Genesis 11, we see mankind all together (not upholding the command to fill the earth), building a tower (the Tower of Babel) to make a name for themselves.

by Diana Gaines

In Genesis 11:6, God says, "If as one people speaking the same language they have begun to do this, then nothing they plan to do will be impossible for them." How could God bring forth His plan for redemption on earth when mankind was pagan and only concerned with making a name for themselves?

Paganism is often described as a group of religions and or spiritual traditions based on a reverence for nature. We can then say a pagan nation is a particular people group who do not know the one true, invisible God personally. Even if these ancient people knew there was a God, they didn't know Him and didn't trust Him. Knowing stuff about God is different than knowing Him as Lord and Savior.

2,000 years from Abraham to Jesus

God's heart is for redemption. He wanted to bring forth a Messiah to once again commune with humanity, but he needed to prepare a people. In order to bring forth His purposes on the earth, God needed a non-pagan nation. Where there is no discipleship there are only pagan nations. God needed to take a people out from the pagan nations, take the pagan practices out of them, and then put them back into the world as a holy nation for the benefit of all the nations. Taking center stage, He began this process by dividing the peoples of the earth through the dispersion of languages (Gen. 11:8).

Now, due to language barriers, people separated and were scattered all over the earth. Years later, a man named Terah set out from Ur of the Chaldeans, heading towards Canaan. We don't know if God called Terah, but we do know God called Abram, Terah's son. Abram, who is later renamed Abraham, is called out: "Leave Your country and your family..." (Gen. 12:1) God then starts the discipleship process and makes a covenant with Abram (Abraham). He declared, "I will make you (Abraham) a great nation... and all the earth will be blessed through you" (Gen. 12:2-3).

Years later at Mount Sinai, God again makes His intentions clear to the nation descended from Abraham: "If you (Israel) obey me fully and keep my covenant, then out of all the nations you will be my treasured possession. You will be for me a holy nation" (Ex. 19:5-6). He then gives His people the loving Ten Commandments and the rest of the law to teach them how to live lives of blessing.

But the Israelites were afraid of the One who loved them the most. They said to Moses, "You speak to us...but do not let God speak to us, lest we die" (Ex. 20:19). Fear and ignorance restrained them from taking the leap of going *all in*. But thankfully, the Holy Spirit had a plan. He was willing to be patient with man and dwelt with them with the hope that one day He would dwell in them.

God reaffirms this in Deuteronomy 14:2. "For you are a people holy to the Lord your God. Out of all the peoples on the face of the earth, the Lord has chosen you to be His treasured possession."

Over a period of 2000 years, the Father brought forth the law and revealed Himself as a God of love, fairness, principle, and order. He did this through:

The Patriarchs

The Prophets

The Apostles

The Messiah

And, most importantly, salvation. "Salvation is from the Jews" (John 4:22).

Every important element in salvation has come through one people group called the Jewish people. In the fullness of time, there was a remnant God could impart His Spirit to because they went through the process of having the world taken out of them. To the degree you allow God to take the world out of you, is to the degree you make room for Christ in you.

33 Years, from Birth to Crucifixion, the Spotlight is on Jesus

The Father took two millennia to establish a nation that could bring forth the Messiah and the early church (apostles and followers of Jesus). After pouring into his disciples for three years, Jesus commands them to "go and make disciples of all nations" (Matt. 28:19). Jesus called Abraham's descendants to go just as God had called Abraham to go. Deliverance from the world is not an end, but preparation for the call of God on our lives.

Thankfully, some Jews did receive Jesus as Messiah and they became the Bible characters of their day. They walked with Jesus, applied His teachings to their lives, and obeyed His command to stay in Jerusalem. Then in Acts 2, as they waited obediently in Jerusalem, they were empowered. Jesus made a way for the Holy Spirit to take center stage as each believer is anointed in the upper room. The tower of Babel is reversed! Instead of confusion, all the Jews who gathered for the Feast of Pentecost hear the good news of Jesus in their own language (15 languages in all).

Did you catch that? Through the anointing of the Holy Spirit, language barriers are removed. God discipled a nation, brought forth the Messiah, and He has now made a way to spread this good news to all peoples! His covenant with Abraham, "all the earth will be blessed through you," is about to come into fuller focus.

Though most of the religious leaders and Abraham's descendants said no to God's call, a few said yes! Out of a population of about 80,000, a remnant of 8,000 went *all in*, and through their obedience and preaching, the New Testament Church was born. It grew among the Jewish people for about 10 years, before the Gentiles were included. Then in Acts 10, Gentiles receive salvation, repentance, and the baptism of the Holy Spirit. Abraham's decedents become a blessing to the nations. The disciples start going into all the world making disciples.

For about 2000 years, from Abraham to Jesus, God discipled the Jewish people to know Him and hold His hand. In the fullness of time, He brought forth the Messiah and entrusted the Jewish people to start His church. In the next 2000 years, Holy Spirit empowers His people, grafts in the gentiles, and all nations are blessed by Abraham's descendants. Now, about 2000 years later, through the Holy Spirit and through technological advances, our world is more connected than ever before. I pray we take this advantage to spread the good news of Jesus and not focus on making a name for ourselves.

Don't miss an important aspect of this dynamic. The Father took two millennia to establish a nation that could bring forth the Messiah. The Messiah was here for only 33 years, and the last three he told us why. "I have prepared a way for the Holy Spirit to dwell in you. It is better that I go away so the Comforter can lead you into all truth." Do you see it? The Father makes a way for the Son and the Son makes a way for the Spirit. There is no competition. The Father, Son, and Holy Spirit are of one heart, one will, securing one end. They are *echod*.

ECHOD

Ready to learn another Hebrew word? Say *Echod* out loud. That's close. It's a really hard *Ekh* (like you're clearing your throat a little), the *a* in tuba, then d (or something close to that). *Echod* means one. One of the most well-known verses to a religious Jew is Deuteronomy 6:4, which is a prayer called the Shema: "Hear, oh Israel, the Lord your God (*Eloheim*), the Lord is *echod* (one)."

Do you remember *Eloheim* (in chapter 5)? These 'Gods' are so united that they are considered one—One Gods. Although they are unique and hold different roles, their hearts are the same, their wills are the same, and they are eternally securing the same end.

The closest thing to compare it to on earth is an ideal marriage. In fact, this same word is used in Genesis when God declares that "a man shall leave his parents and cleave to his wife and become one (*echod*) flesh" (Gen. 2:24). But remember, there is no wickedness or ignorance in God, so their *echod*-ness is far better than the ideal marriage (because humans have limited wisdom and tend to be selfish).

I don't mean to brag, but my marriage is pretty close to ideal. Diana and I intentionally love each other, and we're both committed to the covenant we made to each other. Though I'm far from perfect, we have enjoyed the last forty-plus years a lot. We've held each other's hand through the changes and challenges of life, sharing the same heart, living for the same end, co-created four eternal lives (our kids), and the list goes on. We are very close, but we aren't the same person. Diana and I are both made out of people stuff, but I'm made out of boy stuff, my wife is made out of girl stuff. Our oneness is not in substance but in a covenant relationship with a common unity to ultimately secure the same end.

Knowing stuff about God is different than knowing Him as Lord and Savior.

Likewise, the Father, the Son, and the Holy Spirit are all made out of God stuff, but they are different beings. Though there are differences in manifestation, function, and roles, there is NO distinction in character, motive, and love. They are *echod*—one. If a doctrine teaches there are differences between the attitudes of the Father, Son, and Holy Spirit toward you—it's not biblical. Remember Jesus told his disciples because they've seen Him they've seen the Father (John 14). The Biblical Worldview portrays a Godhead that is echod, in complete unity, fulling their roles in harmony, and constantly honoring each other.

Diana, my wife, is the greatest witness to my life. It's the same in the Godhead. Jesus, the Father, and the Holy Spirit are all the greatest testimonies to each other for all of eternity. Jesus testifies to the Father. The Father testifies: "THIS IS MY SON IN WHOM I'M WELL PLEASED!" The Holy Spirit anoints us with a spirit of revelation to better understand who Jesus and the Father are and how to better relate with them.

NOW GET THIS! This is such a powerful picture of God's love for us. Before the cross, Jesus prayed that we'd have unity with the Father as He does (John 15-17). "That they all may be one, as You, Father, are in Me, and I in You; that they may be one in Us…" (17:21). WOW! God wants to proclaim about me, "This is my son in whom I'm well pleased!" God wants to share the testimony of Himself, from all eternity, with us. He wants to be in an intimate relationship where we are a testimony to each other's lives. I'm not making this up.

The relational dynamic between the Father, Son, and Holy Spirit is the same dynamic God longs for us to have with Him and also with each other. The Holy Spirit never comes up to the Father and questions, "What! Why does Jesus get all the attention?" They're never in competition with each other but always testify of one another. When you have a dynamic like this, within a framework of unity, the power of God can manifest. We as the Body of Christ, the Church, are called to stop infighting and competing, to focus instead on out-blessing each other. When we are unified, when we are *echod*, the world will see God and believe.

What an incredible honor Jesus gives us. He wants us to share in the same *echod*-ness He shares with the Father and the Holy Spirit. THAT'S CRAZY! Let us honor God, respond to this invitation, build our relationship with Him, and experience each relationship in fullness.

Father, thank you for being such an incredible example and making a way for your Son. Thank you, Jesus, for pointing us to the Father and making a way for us to receive the Holy Spirit. Thank you, Holy Spirit, for your patience and empowerment, and leading us deeper into relationship with the Father and the Son.

I want to adopt the generosity of your kingdom and your kindness you show. I want to walk like you. I want to talk like you, think like you, and see the world in the way you see it because you are truly amazing in all of your ways. You are the most strikingly attractive being in the universe and I have now fallen in love with you even deeper than before. Give me your shalom. Remove fear, ideas, and attitudes from my paradigm that prevent me from seeing the world through the eyes of God. Amen.

Download your free *Discussion/Study Guide* for group and individual discipleship. Visit www.kipgaines.com/allin

CHAPTER 11

Covenant

What is an absolute? According to Websters, an absolute is "complete in itself, unconditional, existing independent of any other clause, and not relative." (Websters 1828) Elohim and his covenants are absolute. Though God has created a world with absolutes, He is the only one who is eternally absolute.

Now, there are temporal absolutes. I used to work as a machinist, which a lot of people think is the same as a mechanic. When I joined YWAM, people thought I could fix busses and cars. I was able to fix their vehicles, but machinists actually make machine parts. In my dad's shop, we had these standards called Joe Blocks. These Joe Blocks have to be precise, down the ten-thousandth (.001) of an inch, because they're used for making parts for planes, spaceships, military machines, etc. The parts we made needed to fit exactly with parts created elsewhere. Not only did we have to be precise, but our thermostat in the quality control room needed to be set to 68.5 degrees. Because metal contracts and expands with temperature change, every shop that makes these parts must measure at this temperature. That's the only way to make sure all the pieces fit together when they are later assembled. If a shop did not adhere to the absolute measurement or temperature, their parts would not fit with the others.

Why do we need absolutes? First of all, we need a standard. Like the machinist needs a standard to make sure their particular part will fit with the others, we need a moral standard to know what is good and what's bad. Second, it is essential for our relationship with God. We can not only rest secure in God's abilities but, more importantly, His unwavering character. Even when God shows up and alters cellular structures (walks through walls (John 20:19), interrupts gravity (Acts 1:9), walks on water (Matt. 14), or stops the rotation of the earth (Josh. 10:13)). He and His character are unchanging. The absolutes of physical creation can be altered to reveal His identity, but His love is unchangeable. God is the only eternal absolute, our unwavering reference point, our Father, Friend, and Husband we can count on. Even if your parents forsake you, even if your theology fails, God never will (Ps. 27:10). Elohim and His covenants are absolute.

So, What is Covenant?

Covenant is a relational promise, an agreement, where one or more parties agree to something. When God wants to do something big on the earth, he makes a covenant with someone to bring His purposes into being. He wanted to bring forth a people of faith, so He made a covenant with Abraham. When He wanted to set the Israelites apart as a holy nation and give them the law, He found Moses. Israel cried out for a king, so God set the stage for the Messiah by making a covenant with David. He is a covenant-making, covenant-keeping God who wants to reveal Himself through His people. **By fulfilling His covenant, the Eternal reveals Himself to the temporal.**

God's covenants are absolute. Even if they take thousands of years to accomplish, if God says it, it will come to pass. God said He would make Abraham into a great nation and through his seed all nations would be blessed (Gen. 22:18). Abraham saw the promise of his son Issac fulfilled, but the majority of the Bible is the saga of his family and God's dealings with them. Abraham's family, the Jewish people, did become a great nation. Finally in Matthew 1, we see Jesus, the Messiah, the fulfillment of the covenant, 42 generations (2018 years) later. Despite the wavering faith of His people, God proved He is a covenant-making, covenant-keeping God.

Now, there are two types of covenants, unconditional and conditional. In Deuteronomy, God gives the Israelites both types. He declares unconditionally that Israel will be His people and He will be their God (7:6). There are no conditions here. God wills it and He will do it. But He also gives them the conditional covenant: "If you follow my commands, I will bless you" (Deut. 30). Here the actions of one party determines the others'. If Israel obeys, God's blessings can flow. He makes covenants not only for relationship's sake but to reveal His character and carry out His eternal purposes. The covenant is not an end in itself, but the birthing of a means to an end.

It's also important to note, covenant is not restricted to the extreme mature or the super-spiritual. It has little to do with who you are, your ministry, your gifting, or if you earned it. Israel didn't do anything special to deserve their covenant with God. God needed to disciple a nation to bring forth His promises, so He chose to set His affection upon Israel. He bound Himself to them, and they received. Likewise, with you or me, God is responsible to make and fulfill the covenant, but we do have a part to play. Though God chooses whom to covenant Himself to, we can choose to be prepared or not.

There are two kinds of people in the world. Those who are really grateful and those who are ungrateful. The first kind is far better equipped for covenant than the second. Because we live in a world of five influences and three heavens, we will all experience hardship. Usually, the people who remain grateful through difficulties are victorious and those who don't become victims. Are you victorious or a victim?

A clear contrast between these two mentalities is evident in the Old Testament story of Israel's first two kings. The prophet Samuel anoints Saul to be king. The Bible doesn't give details about Saul's childhood, but we do know he came from a prominent family, he was taller than everyone, and there was none like him (1 Sam. 9). Though Saul was set up for greatness, there were two mindsets that he never overcame. Saul feared man more than God and he wanted to be number one. He was completely wrapped up in himself and what others thought of him. He was a humanist; to him, the end of all being was the happiness of Saul. He had too much esteem for himself and not enough esteem for God. This stance disqualified him, just as it can disqualify others, as a son of covenant. Saul chose not to submit and fully obey God's commands, so God raised up another.

David, on the other hand, is a different story. According to the Bible, it's hard to imagine young David being grateful. He was most likely an illegitimate child. In Psalm 51:5, David wrote: "I was brought forth in iniquity, and in sin did my mother conceive me." This possible illegitimacy could be the reason why he tended sheep and his father did not call him with the rest of his brothers when Samuel came (1 Sam. 16).

If this is true, the reason Jesse didn't call David was because he wanted to hide him. But Jesse's real problem wasn't with David, it was with himself. Jesse was trying to hide himself. Most of the time when people treat you wrongly, it's not because of you, but because they have a problem with themselves. This tends to be true with people who point their finger at God.

Regardless of whether or not David was illegitimate, he often got the short end of the stick. He was stuck with a rough job which kept him isolated and exposed to the elements. Not only was shepherding harsh, but it was also at the bottom of the social ladder. David had every reason to be bitter and angry as he sat out there with his dad's stupid sheep. He could have cursed his situation, nursed a grudge, and rehearsed this horrible hand he was dealt. This attitude would have pushed the call of God right out of his life.

That's a natural reaction, isn't it? When an injustice happens to us, at least from our viewpoint, it's easy to curse it, nurse it, and rehearse it. It brings comfort. Before long, we begin to curse the unjust situation and repeatedly rehearse it in our minds. If this continues long enough, it becomes an obsessive vicious cycle, taking us captive, making escape almost impossible. However, the cycle can be avoided. In the wilderness with the sheep, David resisted this cycle. Because he never formed a grudge, the hardship formed his character and relationship with God. In that season of isolation, David wrote a lot of the Psalms and unknowingly developed skills necessary for his future. He honed his harp skill, which later became his ticket into the royal palace, along with another famous skill.

A good shepherd knows how to protect his sheep. While David was out in the wilderness, he also honed his stone-slinging skills. Why? Well it was common for a wild animal to take a sheep for a snack. Armed with his staff and sling, David probably practiced slinging stones by hitting targets, some smaller predators, and most likely a few sheep by accident. He used his abundance of free time to practice his skill and then tests came. Before fighting Goliath, David recounted his rumbles with a lion and a bear to King Saul (1 Sam. 17).

If David was cursing, nursing, and rehearsing his unfortunate situation, he probably would've just let the lion and bear eat a sheep or two. I mean, they were his dad's sheep, and his dad didn't seem to care about him too much. Screw the old man, right? But David wasn't out there wallowing in self-pity. He was faithful with the task given to him even at risk to his own life. He punched a lion in the face! A lion came after one of his sheep, so David went after it and saved the sheep from its mouth. Later, he faced a bear. Come on! No way would I stick around. They're just sheep! But David runs in, dropkicks this bear, beats the mess out of it, and saves the sheep. More importantly, through it all, he maintains a good attitude.

Thankfully, David honored his father for no apparent reason except for faithfulness to the principles of God and the lack of bitterness in his own heart. This prepared him for God's covenant. He answered the call from his earthly father, which allowed him to receive the call from his Heavenly Father and receive God's anointing. God watched him in the secret place, when no one else was, to see if David was bitter or grateful. Even in the mundane tasks of life attitudes matter; attitudes are a big deal.

This isn't the only place we see evidence of David's exceptional character. After dealing with all those really exciting sheep for however many years and taking out ferocious beasts, David's dad sticks him with another great job. I'm sure you sensed a little sarcasm there.

To set the scene in 1 Samuel 17, David's older brothers are out with Israel's army, standing against the Philistines. And David, well, he stays back with the sheep. David is too young to fight, but he isn't too young to be his dad's mailman. His dad wants news from the battlefront, so he calls for David. "Hey, David. So, I need you to find out how your brothers are doing. It's been a little while since I got an update. I wish they'd deliver the *Hebrew Herald* out here... Anyway, why don't you go check on them? Take them these hunks of cheese, some bread, and bring me back the news. Just put the stuff in the wagon. Sorry, I haven't had a chance to fix that squeaky wheel yet."

Again, David could have cursed, nursed, rehearsed, and refused his dad's request. He could've obeyed begrudgingly and added the stupid squeaky wagon wheel to his list of offenses. But even here, David keeps the right attitude, and his obedience sets the stage for one of the most epic showdowns in history.

Right after David rolls into the Israelite camp <squeak> <squeak> <squeak>, this giant Philistine appears across the valley challenging Israel's army and God. Intimidation overwhelms the whole Israelite army; Goliath is humongous. No one wants to fight this guy. Now Saul, the king, is the obvious choice. He's the leader of the nation and he's a head taller than every other Israelite. Goliath is calling out the whole nation and taunting God, but Saul (and every other soldier) is too afraid to stand up.

If David was cursing, nursing, and rehearsing his unfortunate situation, he would've never faced the giant.

David, who is around thirteen and not even old enough to join the army, can't believe it. He starts yelling, "What will be done for the man who kills this Philistine and removes this disgrace from Israel? Who is this uncircumcised Philistine that he should defy the armies of the living God?" (1 Sam. 17:26). People tell him to shut up. Even his brothers tell him to go back to his sheep. But no one else is willing to fight, so he is taken to Saul. Now remember, Saul is taller than everyone else and the anointed king, but he is afraid. He would rather this kid fight on behalf of his nation. At least he tries to give David his armor, right? David probably looks and feels ridiculous, like a kid wearing his dad's jacket. He can hardly move, much less fight in this getup, so he refuses the normal protection.

How is David so bold? He is ready to go toe to toe with a giant with no traditional protection or weapons. He didn't lay out a fleece. He didn't walk through the principles of guidance (see chapter 3). But David was prepared. He was prepared in the wilderness. He wasn't confident in secret kung fu skills or his stone-slinging skills. He knew the God who was with him in the wilderness. With God, he had killed a lion. With God, he had killed a bear. With God's help, he didn't curse, nurse, and rehearse the hand he was dealt. He wasn't out with the sheep wallowing in self-pity as the central figure of the universe. He worshiped God in the wilderness and that fed the root of purpose and significance instead of the root of bitterness. With God's help, he could kill this Philistine giant. God could bind Himself to David because he wasn't all tied up with his own issues.

If you want to walk away from the purposes of God and destroy your covenant as a son or daughter of God then be judgmental, feed bitterness, and hold unforgiveness. I promise you, your will, will be done and not God's. Critical and judgmental spirits are like rubber bands that hold you back in the journey of life. The more they get on you, the more they pull you back and keep you from the purposes of God. If you want to get from the place God made a promise with you to where that promise is fulfilled you will have to forgive, forgive, forgive.

God prepared David for this moment. God tested him, anointed him, and gave him the confidence to declare, "I ripped a lion's jaw off and punched him in the eye. I drop kicked a bear to save a lamb. That same feeling I had then, I'm having now. I feel it coming all over me. I'm **ALL IN!** I'm going to rip this guy's head off for defying the King of the Universe!" (Kip's paraphrase, 1 Sam. 17:34-37). He felt God's anointing on him, empowering him to run passionately into battle. He knew this giant had no place defying the living God, his God, so David runs into battle. With a sling and a smooth stone, he nails Goliath in the forehead and knocks him out. David then finishes the job by cutting Goliath's head off with the giant's own humongous sword. Even though David is the catalyst for a great victory, he doesn't let the miraculous triumph go to his head because he knows it wasn't his own. This posture, this heart, this obedience, is why God declares that David is a man after His own heart.

Another example of God making covenant with men in the Bible is His covenant with Joshua. He bound Himself to Joshua (Josh. 1) because conflict was imminent, and God wanted His people to walk in fullness. God said, "Be strong and courageous," over and over again because Joshua really needed that encouragement. God prepared him in the wilderness and then anointed him to lead Israel and take the Promised Land. Conflict is inevitable. It's how we learn.

Without conflict, we can never be who God wants us to be. Conflict rightly responded to is a surgical knife that cuts away our carnality and prepares us for the kingdom of God. But naturally, we try to avoid conflict. Most of us would rather walk around the Valley of the Shadow of Death.

Remember Shadrach, Meshach, and Abednego? They were young Israeli captives who were groomed to be advisors in King Nebuchadnezzar's court. They stood with Daniel and didn't let pagan influences corrupt them. In Daniel 3, these three men refused to obey the king's edict to bow down to his statue. Even after they were brought in and reminded about the whole "rebels will be thrown into the fiery furnace" thing, they stood firm, believing God would save them. Like David, they stood up, confident in their God. In a rage, the king ordered the furnace to be cranked up, and these three were thrown in immediately. If I was in their shoes, I'd probably be thinking, "Ok, there's the fire. It's really hot. Anytime now God…" Whether or not these guys thought something similar, they declared the ultimate intention of their hearts. They made it clear they won't put anyone or anything before their God, and they were ready to die if God didn't intervene (Dan. 3:16-18).

The fire isn't comfortable. This fire, in particular, was so hot the heat alone kills the guards who tossed in the trio. Now, God could've intervened before they were thrown in the fire, but that wasn't His highest. His highest was for these three to walk through the fire.

While they are IN the fire, the king looked in and said, "Weren't there three men that we tied up and threw into the fire? I see four men walking around in the fire, unbound and unharmed, and the fourth looks like a son of the gods" (Dan. 3:25). Though we'd rather skip the furnace altogether, our most intimate, powerful meetings with Jesus are in the midst of the fire. Without death, there can be no resurrection. If we really believe God is who He says He is, who cares how hot that furnace is? In fact, the hotter it is the greater the miracle. We can be sure that, just as He was with these three, Jesus is with us in the fire.

In the New Testament, Jesus made a covenant with the disciples, but they certainly had problems. There was selfish ambition, naivety, betrayal, and spiritual impotence to name a few. On a couple of occasions, the disciples jockeyed for position ("Who's the greatest?" Matt. 18). They often didn't seem to get what Jesus was talking about, what his actions meant, and were rebuked for their lack of faith. Judas Iscariot wasn't the only betrayer. They all asked, "Is it I?" during the last supper, and they all deserted Him after He was arrested.

God doesn't choose the most perfect. He usually chooses the most willing but not always. When Jesus got ready to build the church, he made some strange choices. He left the job of spreading the Gospel to eleven guys that weren't exactly the cream of the crop. I wouldn't have picked some of them. But if I'm honest, I wouldn't pick me either.

The disciples had covenant then they failed. Did covenant fail? NO! God's word doesn't fail. Even when we fail, the covenant is still good. My hope is in Jesus' love, not my love. The disciples backslid, even after Jesus was resurrected. Remember from the last chapter? They went back to fishing in John 21 and not for morning recreation. The original language implies their intentions were to return to their previous profession. This didn't catch Jesus off guard. In fact, Jesus prophesied during the last supper that He would meet them back in Galilee (Matt. 26:32).

He met them there on the shores of Galilee and restored them, specifically Peter. Jesus is committed to the covenants He makes. Covenant is less about who you are than who God is. There are many stories of men and women who are called by God, backslide, then finally come back, and God still fulfills His purposes. Covenant is the fulfillment of what Jesus wants to bring forth in our lives. Covenant is about who God is, a covenant-making, covenant-keeping God.

The disciples were sifted, as are all true followers of God. Tests—or the crucible of life—refine us and turn us hunks of coal into diamonds. This natural process for diamonds to form requires time and pressure. It's the same in the spiritual. The pressures of life and time in the wilderness transformed David. The pressure and the forty years in the wilderness formed Joshua. It was the pressure of captivity and assimilation into a pagan culture for Shadrach and company, not to mention the literal fire. The same is needed for our transformation. If we respond rightly under the pressure of conflict, in time we too can become diamonds.

If you got what you deserve, where would you spend eternity? Take a moment to think about it. Eternally separated from God. Do you really believe that or is it just an abstract concept? Does this truth affect you? Does it affect the way you live at all? Many people say they believe, but their theology doesn't actually change the way they live. If your "belief" does not affect your actions, it's just an idea—not really a belief. An idea has consequences when it becomes a belief. If we really and truly believed the ideas we have, how different would our lives be?

Studying the Bible, going to church, or praying is essential to our growth, but that's all secondary to how much Jesus gets into you. This amount is not determined by time devoted to practices or programs. It's determined by you, as a son or daughter. Jesus saves us with the full intention of entering into a covenant relationship with us, like a marriage. His heart is not for us to continually get divorced and remarried but to walk through the changes and challenges of life holding his hand, never letting go.

When God wants to do something on the earth, He binds Himself to someone. Why? Because if that person is going to walk out what God showed them, they are going to need God. God wants to make a covenant with you. He's searching, watching, and testing to find out who is going to be humble, broken, and ready to make a covenant relationship with Him. He then finds a partner to bring forth His plans and purposes on the earth. God's heart is to reveal Himself to the world. That is why He binds Himself to men. That's why He makes covenant.

> *When God wants to do something on the earth,*
> *He binds Himself to someone.*

God has plans, intentions, passions, and purposes. He's doing something on the earth. He's not going to quit binding Himself to men, He's only begun. I think we are going to see the fire of God in the last days as we've never seen before. God is raising up an army of men and women who will get over the little stuff, embrace the purposes of God, and be the greatest world changers ever to walk the face of the earth. I don't think it has to do with qualifications or giftings but everything to do with covenant.

Whenever we focus on ourselves, Jesus is pushed out. Whenever we focus on Jesus, our selfishness is pushed out. The world doesn't revolve around me. It revolves around something so much more beautiful than me. Something so much more valuable than me. Something so much bigger than me. God invites me, and you, to be a part of this grand story. This life isn't about receiving the love of God that puffs up the value of man. It's about lavishing love upon the Son of God, so He can reveal His promises and Himself through His covenants. If you want Jesus to be highly esteemed, then you're in the place where you can decrease, and He can increase. You are prepared to walk in covenant.

If that's YOU, my dear friend, you are ready to go ALL IN!

Download your free *Discussion/Study Guide* for group and individual discipleship. Visit wwwkipgaines.com/allin

CHAPTER 12

No Turning Back

The Marriage Ceremony—Part I

When you were little, others praised you for doing the smallest things. Seriously, people went crazy for you just taking a step. "Oh look! Come look! Oooh, ooh! A step! You did so good!"

Now you're older. You don't get praise for taking a step. Those little things aren't impressive anymore. No one applauds you for things that you're expected to do. You've grown and so have the expectations of you.

When you first get saved, and start walking out of your sinful life, God gets real excited over our simple obedience. Remember the Parable of the Prodigal Son? The Father threw a party just because His son came back home. Sure, that's awesome, but it can't end there. Coming home is only the beginning of walking in fullness. God expects us to mature in our faith. He has hopes, desires, dreams for you that can only be accomplished as you walk in covenant with Him.

This Christianity thing isn't a correctional institution to improve behavior, it's relational. It's holding God's hand. It's about walking in covenant. As we walk and grow with God, we're called to take on bigger and bigger challenges. These challenges are too big for us by design. We're screwed if we don't hold His hand.

God calls His followers the Bride of Christ. Have you ever thought of those implications? Marriage represents a defining moment where everything changes! It begins a supernatural process. The goal is not to make us the best version of ourselves; we are called to something greater than ourselves! When you enter into covenant, when you marry Jesus, you start a process to become what Jesus and you can become together.

During our journey, we may experience a "dark night of the soul." Our only security in these times is our marriage commitment to God. If we are committed, even the darkest moments erupt into a greater bond with our Creator, the Author and Perfector of our faith (Heb. 12).

I believe with all my heart that our confidence in covenant relationship with God is 90% God and about 10% us. He says that He will hold our hand through the changes and challenges of life and never let go. All He requires of us is that we commit to holding His hand as we walk through life and never let go.

This final chapter will package all the concepts, truths, and (most of all) relational dynamics described in the previous chapters into our marriage experience as His bride. Before I get to the marriage ceremony, I want to share a journal entry I wrote while living in the Middle East after being in covenant relationship and ministry with the Lord for 30 years.

Journaling: Israel, Nov 13, 2013 (by Kip Gaines)

During extended water fast: weak, vulnerable, emotional, and disappointed in myself.

Once again trying to understand forgiveness, love, and atonement in light of the fear of the Lord. God is great, and I am so frail. Why am I so blind to some realities?

When I engage in life, I experience friendship with God and walk in His anointing. I feel overwhelming gratitude, aware that I'm special because God is my friend. At the same time, I can experience feelings of inadequacy and insecurity. This seems to be the condition I abide in at times.

Then I blow it. I blunder and commit sin either by ignorance or self-indulgence. I'm influenced by my emotions or fall prey to a demonic influence. I find myself saying or doing something stupid—again.

When this happens, the world seems to change. The joy of walking in the anointing of the Lord is drowned out by a preoccupation of my blunder. My spirit is open to all sorts of accusations and fear begins to paralyze me. The declaration over my future becomes: "I know the plans I have for you, plans to steal from you, kill you, and bring despair, rejection, and hopelessness. Plans for self-hatred, shame, self-pity, self-medication, and finally DEATH!"

But I know the Lord says in Jeremiah 29:11, "For I know the plans I have for you, declares the Lord, plans to prosper you and not to harm you, plans to give you hope and a future. Then you will call upon me and find me when you search for me with all your heart."

My battle begins with this contrast because I'm sure I'm done for—especially this time. There's no hope of repair, I fear the Holy Spirit is disappointed and somewhat lifted the anointing. Now my existence with God is reduced to a relationship without clarity of thought or anointing to produce something of impacting value. I'm too intimidated and aware of my unworthiness. Things seem quite bleak! The enemy really has a stronghold. The depth of my despair has reached critical levels, almost to the point of abandoning my post. I cry out to my Savior and ask forgiveness—again.

Then tenderness of the Lord comes, with radical, clearly drawn boundaries. These are the same past boundaries I've been unable to carry out in the flesh! I can't do it on my own. I come to the end of myself and cry out.

"Save me! Save me, oh God! I just want to be like you. I want to think like you, I want to talk like you, I want to walk like you, I want to feel the way you feel, experience what you do, and see the world through your eyes!"

Then, I sense a flood of hope. My blunder or sin may not be my ruin. The blood of Jesus can cleanse and heal and restore.

There are times the response of men can be so encouraging and release such an influence. It's like God sending them to protect me. However, other times my wounded soul is wounded even deeper through the comments of men, adding insult to injury. Then I respond in a reactionary way, taking on rejection, hurt, shame, or the worst possible attitude—unforgiveness or resentment. These are totally contrary to the love of God!

I find myself right back where I began! Oh, God what is the answer to this dilemma?

Receiving God's forgiveness and releasing forgiveness to anyone who offends me:

- Puts God in right perspective.
- Puts God on the throne of my life.
- Puts God in a position above my limits.

- Puts God above my personal comfort.
- Puts God above my earthly relationships.
- Puts God above my insecurities and fears.
- Puts God as my today—to presently live and move in Him.
- Puts God as my tomorrow—with a hope and a future.
- Puts me out of the hands of men and ushers me into the hands of God!

This! This is what I want! Why does it escape me? I have it in part, but I need more. I'm desperate for the fullness! Where deep cries out to deep!!

I want forgiveness and the fear of the Lord to govern my every thought, move, and attitude. To be my life! To be who I am!

What brings this radical climax of receiving the forgiveness and fear of the Lord? LOVE. Liquid love demonstrated through the cross!

Jacob saw Rachel, the way God views me! "And Jacob served seven years for Rachel; and they seemed unto him but a few days, for the love he had to her" (Gen. 29:20).

Love endures all things (1 Cor. 13:7).

When we are in love, no sacrifice is too great!

Serving is a joy!

Being together is all that matters.

Sleep is not so necessary.

I'd travel a billon miles just to be with you!

Adrenaline overcomes bodily weariness.

Sacrifice? What sacrifice? I want to do it.

Oh no, it's ok. All these accommodations are fine.

Come on! When we are in love, everything changes. From the twitterpated boy/girl love to honoring someone you respect. From the agape love of knowing God to receiving forgiveness through extending forgiveness—**Love changes everything!!**

This love feeling doesn't last forever at the same intensity or resolve. Sometimes it gets stronger and matures—more powerful than before. Sometimes it grows weaker, even though I wish it to grow stronger.

I'm told love is not a special way of feeling. But when I do feel it, life and ministry are so much more gratifying to my Spirit, my relationships, my outlook, and my ability to maintain all of life.

God, help me understand how forgiveness and the fear of the Lord must be established in my every thought! I want Philippians 4:8 to be the grid I see the world through.

"Finally, brothers and sisters, whatever is true, whatever is noble, whatever is right, whatever is pure, whatever is lovely, whatever is admirable—if anything is excellent or praiseworthy—think about such things" (Phil 4:8). That's what I want!

When I come to you, Jesus, I rely on what you did on the cross. No longer is my sin in the forefront of my mind. Lucifer is not able to use my blunders as a filter for all my thoughts and relationships. My preoccupation based on condemnation in an awful existence disappears, and I realize that "You were pierced through for our transgression and crushed for our iniquities. The chastening for our well-being fell upon You and by Your scourging we are healed" (Isa. 53:5).

Jesus! Take my sin, my failure, my rejection, my shame, take this attack of the enemy and REPLACE IT WITH THE HOLY SPIRIT!

Friendship—Freedom—Purpose

For me, it is just too much. There is not enough love, gratitude, expression of lifestyle, or long enough period of time to adequately express my heart.

Thank You! I SO LOVE YOU! You gave it all! What, as the bride, can I give? I receive the gift of forgiveness, and I want to extend forgiveness as a witness to Your life!

When I receive forgiveness and forgive, my main focal point becomes—I just want to be with You, be like You, know You, and see the world through Your eyes!

I'm able to process the origins of thought that enter my mind, harness those thoughts, and actually have the mind of Christ.

The Spirit of the Lord, the most precious gift, will rest upon me and I can delight in the fear of the Lord (Isa. 11: 2–3). In the presence of the Lord there is fullness of joy! (Ps. 16:11). God, I love your presence!

Jesus, I cry out! Let us be *ECHOD*! Just as You and the Father are one!

I long to be so intimate with you that every thought would be captured and enraptured with love for you! That every thought would be baptized in the anointing of discernment and fear of the Lord!

I want to think like You, talk like You, walk like You; see the world through Your eyes, so I can have the mind of Christ and be an imitator of You! *ECHOD!*

So, I renounce the spirits and any lofty thought that has raised itself up against the love of God (2 Cor. 10:5)! Forgive me my transgressions as I forgive those who transgressed against me (Matt. 6).

I am a sinner, and I come before You God and ask for Your forgiveness. As I receive this gift of forgiveness, I release total forgiveness to anyone You bring to my mind, who asks for forgiveness, and especially those who have transgressed against me.

I give to you the loss of finances, disappointment, self-hatred, my severe pain and health issues, betrayal of friends, and insecurities of the present. I even give you my inability to think clearly and overcome temptation! I surrender it all to you!

All things. All things! All things work together for good to them that love God, to them who are called to His purposes (Rom. 8:28). God, you are who you say you are! Do what You see as best, God. I don't always understand, but God, I trust you!

Abba, I trust you! **I receive your forgiveness!**

The Marriage Ceremony—Part II

God doesn't just give us the opportunity to become His bride, this is what the Christian walk is all about. "This is eternal life, that they may know you" (John 17:3). To walk with God, to *ginosko* Him, we must mature past the little steps. He's called each of us to an intimate, covenant relationship. And unforgiveness is not an option.

When you are married, you become more like your spouse. When I got married, I became more like Diana, and she became more like me. Our standards change. This can be a problem if our partner's standard is too high. Many people get frustrated in their walk with Jesus when they realize they can't possibly live up to His standard. Some give up, while others compromise. But guess what?! Jesus wants to have deep intimacy with us, so He makes a way. He is willing to patiently carry us through the process of transformation to become a pure and spotless bride.

His forgiveness makes a way for us to become more like Him. Sadly, we tend to hold onto things like offense, guilt, and bondage. These keep us from receiving and extending forgiveness. If we want to walk in fullness, if we want to be the bride, we must meet one condition. We must forgive. We must forgive to be forgiven (Matt. 6:15).

Why? God wants us to become like Him and think like Him. He wants us to do in minimum what He does in magnitude. We must have the mind of God to walk with God—that's the Sermon on the Mount. Forgiveness is a decision to obey God and walk in a way that highlights what Jesus did on the cross. Forgiveness is the only way we can be free.

Because of the cross, we're not beholden to others' attitudes and actions. You can move in the opposite spirit and be an unrestricted channel to release the love of God to all those around you—to your mom, dad, leaders, and anyone else who treated you inappropriately. They aren't accountable to you; don't stay in bondage. When you forgive (decide to obey) you walk in a higher realm.

It's ok if we don't fully understand. God spoke and everything came into being. Really?! There are some big things way beyond our comprehension, but God gives us a little requirement to be in relationship with Him. We must receive the fullness of forgiveness so we're willing to extend forgiveness to anyone who wrongs us.

Before I go on, I want to acknowledge one of my biggest challenges in discipling others. So many misunderstand true forgiveness. I've counseled many deeply wounded people who didn't want to be put back into vulnerable situations. This is very common, so let me explain:

What forgiveness is not:

- Forgiveness is not a feeling—it is a choice I make.
- Forgiveness is not pretending you were not hurt.
- Forgiveness is not saying they weren't wrong.
- Forgiveness is not saying you can or need to ever trust that person again.
- Forgiveness is not removing responsibility for another's attitudes or actions.

Hopefully, this understanding removes any stumbling blocks keeping us from the incredible life-giving freedom of experiencing and exercising forgiveness. But now, how can we actually do this thing? We must consider and follow what the Bible teaches so our forgiveness is genuine.

How to practice forgiveness:

- Acknowledge it is a biblical absolute.
- Admit you have the need to forgive.
- Admit you need to be restored.
- Ask the Father to restore you.
- Receive God's method, timing, and ways of walking you through administering His forgiveness.

Forgiveness is the surgical knife that removes the barrier that separates us from this covenant communion with God and even with other people. If you choose not to forgive for any reason, then what you are saying by inference is, "What that person did to you is more important to you than going on with God." Forgiveness is a decision I make to obey God and to walk as a lifestyle in a higher realm, reflecting what Jesus did on the cross for me!

It takes both receiving and extending forgiveness to make our relationship with God possible. Our great privilege is that God will never bring up our sin again. Jesus never reminds us that we blew it.

That's incredible, isn't it? God extends this privilege because He loves us. Because he loves us, Jesus emptied himself (Phil. 2:7). While still being God, He lived his life as a man led by the Holy Spirit and not doing His own will first.

This is *kenosis* in Greek. Jesus surrendered Himself and His attributes;

He was emptied His own intrinsic powers, privileges, and protection. God compressed into a human (Col. 2:9). Somehow the infinite Jesus becomes a man. His emptying transcends far beyond our understanding. He is King of kings, but JESUS BECAME FORGIVENESS IN BODILY FORM!

How do we respond to such extravagance?

Go ALL IN. Are you ready?

If you are, I want to encourage you to prepare communion for this last part. I'm not kidding. Put the book down. Go get a piece of bread or a cracker. Pour a small cup of wine, grape juice, or whatever, and then come back. If you are serious, if you want to seal this covenant with God, if you want to marry Jesus, then I want to invite you to take communion as you read this final part.

Are you ready? Now, with communion, let's read this passage. Remember Jesus' forgiveness and His sacrifice to make this covenant relationship possible.

> *While they were eating, Jesus took some bread, and after a blessing, He broke it and gave it to the disciples, and said, "Take, eat; this is My body."*

> *And when He had taken a cup and given thanks, He gave it to them, saying, "Drink from it, all of you; for this is My blood of the covenant, which is poured out for many for the forgiveness of sins. But I say to you, I will not drink of this fruit of the vine from now on until that day when I drink it new with you in My Father's kingdom."*

I can't wait to do this, you guys! It's going to be incredible!

> *After singing a hymn, they went out to the Mount of Olives. Then Jesus said to them, "You will all fall away because of Me this night, for it is written, 'I will strike down the shepherd, and the sheep of the flock shall be scattered.' But after I have been raised, I will go ahead of you to Galilee."*

> *But Peter said to Him, "Even though all may fall away because of You, I will never fall away."*

> *Jesus said to him, "Truly I say to you that this very night before a rooster crows, you will deny Me three times."*

> *Peter said to Him, "Even if I have to die with You, I will not deny You." All the disciples said the same thing too.*

Then Jesus came with them to a place called Gethsemane, and said to His disciples, "Sit here while I go over there and pray."

And He took with Him Peter and the two sons of Zebedee and began to be grieved and distressed. Then He said to them, "My soul is deeply grieved, to the point of death; remain here and keep watch with Me."

And He went a little beyond them, and fell on His face and prayed, saying, "My Father, if it is possible, let this cup pass from Me; yet not as I will, but as You will."

And He came to the disciples and found them sleeping, and said to Peter, "So, you men could not keep watch with Me for one hour? Keep watching and praying that you may not enter into temptation; the spirit is willing, but the flesh is weak."

He went away again a second time and prayed, saying, "My Father, if this cannot pass away unless I drink it, Your will be done."

Again, He came and found them sleeping, for their eyes were heavy. And He left them again, and went away and prayed a third time, saying the same thing once more.

Then He came to the disciples and said to them, "Are you still sleeping and resting? Behold, the hour is at hand and the Son of Man is being betrayed into the hands of sinners. Get up, let us be going; behold, the one who betrays Me is at hand!" (Matt. 26:26-46)

Before we take communion, I want to point out something very important. Jesus tells His disciples that Satan has demanded to sift them like wheat, but He has prayed for them. When they go to Gethsemane, He tells them, "Stay here, watch and pray that you do not fall into temptation."

Can you grasp the fullness of God's love? We can't—but try to grasp it a little more. Up until this point Jesus' concerns are clearly for His friends. He takes three disciples further and tells them He's exceedingly sorrowful and grieved, even to the point of death. Then He goes a stone's throw further and prays that this cup pass from Him. Then He goes back to the disciples and gives the same admonition "watch and pray that *you* don't enter into temptation." He returns to *prayer*, then back to *them* with the same admonition. Back to *prayer*, back *to them*, and then He is betrayed.

Three times He told them to watch and pray so *they* don't enter into temptation because Satan has demanded to sift *them* as wheat. Can you see Jesus is not worried about Himself? And the Bible isn't exaggerating the extent He's crying out for His disciples; "to the point of death." The fact is, they're all He's thinking about. He is pouring out His heart in intercession!

This intercession becomes so intense, He sheds blood and wonders if He might die of hypothermia and shock. He asks His Father to remove this cup of death so that He can reveal the Father's broken heart to us, through His death, even on a cross!

I personally believe Jesus, our Good Shepherd, prays alone here because He is interceding for the one who is being sifted as wheat at that very moment—Judas. He loved Judas. In the scriptures, Jesus never enters into self-pity. But He was, however, overwhelmed with grief! Grief is proportionate to a desire for intimacy lost. Grief is totally different from self-pity. His attention was on others, not on Himself. His grief and sorrow are for Judas' blindness and stupidity of refusing forgiveness. God wishes that none should perish (2 Peter 3:9). Judas, and the religious leaders, just don't get it. They're not just preparing to kill God. Their sin is destroying themselves and they are perishing. The more comprehension we have of eternity, the deeper the sense of loss and grief will be!

What took place in the garden reveals Jesus' great love for me—for you. No matter what we've done, He still desires intimacy and calls us forth as His bride! Yeshua loves us even when we reject His forgiveness, even as He was lifted with outstretched arms! "Father, forgive them, they know not what they do!" (Luke 23:34). He came while we were yet sinners—this is the gospel of Jesus Christ.

With this fresh reminder, let's go back to Matthew 26:26-29, as Jesus prepares communion.

> *While they were eating, Jesus took some bread, and after a blessing, He broke it and gave it to the disciples, and said, "Take, eat; this is My Body."*

Take the bread.

> *And when He had taken a cup and given thanks, He gave it to them, saying, "Drink from it, all of you; for this is My blood of the covenant, which is poured out for many for the forgiveness of sins. But I say to you, I will not drink of this fruit of the vine from now on until that day when I drink it new with you in My Father's kingdom."*

Take the wine. IMAGINE! We are going to do this in heaven! We are going to commune with Jesus, with the Father, and drink that new wine together! Incredible!

Remember this emptying of Himself, this sacrifice was Jesus' joy. It was His joy, because He desires you and me to be his bride, filled with the Holy Spirit, and walking with Him. "For the joy set before him…" (Heb. 12:2).

"He is not here, for He has risen, just as He said. Come, see the place where He was lying." (Matt. 28:6)

"Therefore, Jesus being by the right hand of God exalted, and having received of the Father the promise of the Holy Ghost, he hath shed forth this, which ye now see and hear (Acts 2:33).

He lives in us. Christ in us hope of glory (Col. 1:27).

Let us be glad and rejoice and give honor to him: for the marriage of the Lamb is come, and his wife has made herself ready. And to her was granted that she should be arrayed in fine linen, clean and white: For the fine linen is the righteousness of saints. And he saith unto me, "Write, blessed are they which are called unto the marriage supper of the Lamb." And he saith unto me, "These are the true sayings of God" (Rev. 19:7-9).

God is asking: Will you be one with Him? Will you commit and walk in covenant with the Creator?

I do. I take communion and receive the seal of this marriage covenant between myself and God. As God is calling forth His Bride, I say:

Here am I. I'm ALL IN.

WANT TO HELP US SHARE THIS TRUTH?

Thanks for giving us the opportunity to share **All In** with you. Our prayer (and we believe God's desire) is that the truth in this book would impact as many lives as possible.

Please help reach more readers by leaving us an honest review wherever you purchased this book. THANKS!

So appreciate your help!

Blessings, Kip and Will

www.ingramcontent.com/pod-product-compliance
Lightning Source LLC
Chambersburg PA
CBHW030312130626
46549CB00002B/823